1st Century AD

Roman Soldier

VERSUS

Germanic Warrior

COMBAT

Lindsay Powell

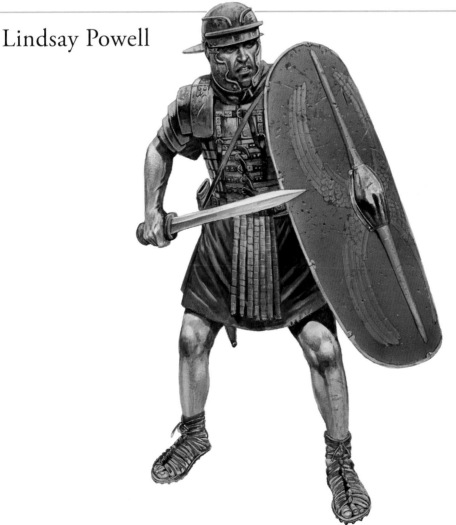

First published in Great Britain in 2014 by Osprey Publishing,
PO Box 883, Oxford, OX1 9PL, UK
PO Box 3985, New York, NY 10185-3985, USA
Email: info@ospreypublishing.com

Osprey Publishing, part of Bloomsbury Publishing Plc.

A CIP catalogue record for this book is available from the British Library

Print ISBN: 978 1 4728 0349 8
PDF ebook ISBN: 978 1 4728 0350 4
ePub ebook ISBN: 978 1 4728 0351 1

Index by Alan Thatcher
Typeset in Univers, Sabon and Adobe Garamond Pro
Maps and diagrams by bounford.com
Artwork by Peter Dennis
Originated by PDQ Media, Bungay, UK
Printed in China through World Print Ltd.

17 18 19   11 10 9 8 7 6 5 4

Osprey Publishing is supporting the Woodland Trust, the UK's leading
woodland conservation charity, by funding the dedication of trees.

www.ospreypublishing.com

Author's acknowledgements

For their help in providing photographs which illustrate this volume
I would like to thank: Chris Haines MBE, Mike Knowles and the
members of The Ermine Street Guard in the United Kingdom; Dan
Dalby, Tony Austin and the members of Project Germani in British
Columbia, Canada; and Jasper L. Oorthuys and Dr Josho Brouwers of
Ancient Warfare magazine in The Netherlands. This book is dedicated to
the community of archaeologists, conservators and re-enactors who keep
alive the memory of the past and, through their work of excavation,
preservation, interpretation and reconstruction, reveal anew the
astonishing skill and creativity of our ancient ancestors.

Author's note

The dating convention used throughout is the *Anno Domini* designation
of BC/AD. Quotations from ancient sources are adapted from the Loeb
Classical Library. Unless otherwise accredited, all images are from the
author's personal collection.

Artist's note

Readers may care to note that the original paintings from which
the plates of this book were prepared are available for private sale.
All reproduction copyright whatsoever is retained by the Publishers.
All inquiries should be addressed to:

Peter Dennis, 'Fieldhead', The Park, Mansfield, Nottinghamshire
NG18 2AT, UK, or email magie.h@ntlworld.com

The Publishers regret that they can enter into no correspondence upon
this matter.

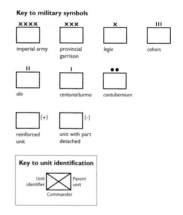

Key to military symbols

imperial army | provincial garrison | legio | cohors

ala | centuria/turma | contubernium

reinforced unit (+) | unit with part detached (-)

Key to unit identification

Unit identifier | Parent unit | Commander

Editor's note

Distances and weights are quoted in present-day 'imperial' measures throughout: see the conversion table below for Roman and metric equivalents.

Roman unit	English name	Equivalent to	English equivalent	Metric equivalent
pes	Roman foot	1 *pes*	0.972ft*	296.3mm*
–	foot	–	1ft	304.8mm
mille passuum, milliarum	Roman mile	5,000 *pedes*	4,854ft (0.919 standard mile)	1.479km
–	mile	–	1 mile	1.609km
As, libra	Roman pound	1 *libra*	0.725lb	328.9g
–	pound	–	1lb	453.6g
–	ton	–	1 ton	1,016kg

* Based on the foot on the statue of Pan signed by Marcus Cossutius Cerdo from a villa at Monte Cagnolo, near Rome, Italy now in the British Museum, GR 1805.7-3.28-29 (Sculpture 1666–67). Alternative modern assessments suggest that a *pes* was equivalent to 0.971ft (295.9mm) or 0.986ft (300.5mm).

CONTENTS

Introduction

'Who would leave Asia, or Africa, or Italia for Germania, with its wild country, its inclement skies, its sullen manners and aspect, unless indeed it were his home?' (Tacitus, *Germania* 2). This negative perception of Germania – the modern Netherlands and Germany – lay behind the reluctance of Rome's great military commanders to tame its immense wilderness. Caius Iulius Caesar famously threw a wooden pontoon bridge across the River Rhine (*Rhenus*) in just ten days, not once but twice, in 55 and 53 BC. The next Roman general to do so was Marcus Agrippa, in 39/38 BC or 19/18 BC. However, none of these missions was for conquest, but in response to pleas for assistance from an ally of the Romans, the Germanic nation of the Ubii. It was not until the reign of Caesar Augustus that a serious attempt was made to annex the land beyond the wide river and transform it into a province fit for Romans to live in. Successive explorations had established its boundaries:

> Germania is separated from the Galli, the Raeti, and Pannonii, by the rivers *Rhenus* and *Danuvius* [Danube]; mountain ranges, or the fear which each feels for the other, divide it from the Sarmatae and Daci. Elsewhere ocean girds it, embracing broad peninsulas and islands of unexplored extent, where certain tribes and kingdoms are newly known to us, revealed by war. (Tacitus, *Germania* 1)

However, its scale eluded the geographers of the Ancient World, including the best minds Agrippa had brought together to compile a 'Map of the World' (*Orbis Terrarum*):

> … the dimensions of its respective territories it is quite impossible to state, so immensely do the authors differ who have touched upon this subject. The Greek writers and some of our own countrymen have stated the coast of Germania to be 2,500 miles in extent, while Agrippa, comprising Raetia and Noricum in his estimate, makes the length to be 686 miles, and the breadth 148. (Pliny the Elder, *Natural History* 4.28)

Such inaccurate measurements made military planning problematic from the outset. When compared to Agrippa's combined measurement of the three conquered provinces of Aquitania, Belgica and Gallia Comata or 'Long Haired Gaul' (420 Roman miles long by 318 miles wide), the whole of Germania was only eight times greater. It had taken the army of Iulius Caesar just nine years to reduce these Three Gallic Provinces (*Tres Galliae*). Hispania had taken 200 years. On that basis the conquest of Germania seemed an attainable objective.

The land was inhabited by a patchwork of tribal nations (*nationes*). The Romans referred to them collectively as *Germani*, but they identified themselves by tribal names. Some – like the Sugambri – were related to the Iron Age Celts who inhabited Gaul, while others, such as the Cherusci, shared a different cultural and linguistic tradition called Germanic. Some nations were ruled by kings, while others were collectives that elected their leaders. Most people lived relatively independently with their families on farms, rather than in towns, though at least one is known: Mattium, the capital of the Chatti (the location of which remains obscure).

During the reign of Augustus (27 BC–AD 14), the basic unit of the Roman Army (*exercitus*) was the legion, derived from the Latin word *legio* meaning 'military levy'. Soldiers (*legionarii*) for the army were recruited exclusively from male citizens principally from Italy, but their numbers were increasingly augmented by volunteers (*volones*) from the provinces. There were 28 legions of 5,600–6,000 men each in service at the start of AD 9. Additionally there were elite Praetorian Cohorts – initially nine, but rising to 12 in the later part of Augustus' principate – perhaps representing 12,000 men in all, located at camps around Italy. To supplement the ranks of the Roman legions, non-citizen allies from outside the empire were recruited and formed their own units (*alae, cohortes*) of 500 or 1,000 men each. These ethnic auxiliary

In 17 BC an alliance of Tencteri and Usipetes nations led by warchief Maelo of the Sugambri raided into the Roman province of Gallia Belgica. Encountering them by chance, the governor Marcus Lollius was ambushed and the eagle standard of *Legio* V *Alaudae* was captured by the Germans. The event became known as the *Clades Lolliana* – 'Lollian Disaster'. It was the trigger for Caesar Augustus to embark on a re-assessment of north-western border security, leading to the conception of a war to annex Germania. This 19th-century painting by Friedrich Tüshaus romantically evokes a clash on the banks of the Rhine between the Roman Army and Germanic warriors, complete with anachronistic winged helmets. (Public domain)

Nero Claudius Drusus (Drusus the Elder) led the first serious attempt at conquering Germania for the Romans. In preparation for his campaigns in 14 BC he founded legionary fortresses whose locations on the Rhine became permanent bases and then important cities of the empire, and have survived to our own day. After his death following a riding accident in 9 BC, the Senate posthumously awarded him the honorary war title *Germanicus*, meaning 'the German' or 'of Germania'. His sons were permitted to adopt the title. This gold *aureus* was minted by his youngest son, Emperor Claudius. (Harlan J. Berk. Author's collection)

troops were particularly important for providing specialist infantry, such as archers (*sagittarii*) from Crete and cavalry (*turmae*) from the foothills of the Alps. Several Germanic nations served the Roman army in this capacity, often under their own chiefs. Among them were the Batavi, Chauci, Cherusci, Frisii, Sugambri and Ubii. The exact number of auxiliary units in service at the start of AD 9 is not known, but they made up about half of Rome's total military forces.

A permanent fleet of ships (*classis*) for sea patrols was based at Misenum on the Bay of Naples to patrol the sea-lanes used by grain ships sailing between Italy, Africa, Sicily and Egypt. A fleet was located at Ravenna, which patrolled the Adriatic coastline, and another – established by Drusus the Elder in 13 or 12 BC – operated from several bases along the Rhine to assist the army of Germania with its operations. At full strength the combined manpower of legionary, Praetorian, auxiliary and marine forces may have amounted to 300,000–330,000. In AD 9 about one third were stationed at forts along the Rhine or its tributaries. Rome's emerging German province and its borderlands were home to a diverse community of many different nations.

The catalyst for the outright conquest of Germania appears to be a raid by an alliance of German nations under the leadership of Maelo of the Sugambri, in 17 BC. By chance they encountered and ambushed the Roman governor (*legatus Augusti pro praetore*) and his *Legio* V *Alaudae*, taking the legion's eagle standard (*aquila*) as a trophy. The humiliation became known as the 'Lollian Disaster' (*Clades Lolliana*). The following year Augustus replaced his governor with his eldest stepson (and future emperor) Tiberius Claudius Nero, and joined him in person in Gaul to carry out an assessment and lay down plans for war. In preparation for it, in 15 BC Augustus' youngest stepson, Nero Claudius Drusus (Drusus the Elder), was given command of an army and with it he annexed the territory of the Raeti in northern Italy and the central Alps, and that of the Vindelici in the Bavarian Voralpenland. The next year Drusus the Elder assumed the governorship of the Three Gallic Provinces and with it responsibility for prosecuting the war in Germania.

In one of the largest construction projects of the Augustan Age, Drusus' legionaries spent two backbreaking years building military infrastructure comprising five legionary fortresses and a connecting road along the Rhine, a system of canals (*fossa Drusiana*) connecting the river to the *Lacus Flevo* (Zuiderzee/IJsselmeer) and a fleet of tubby barges and troop transports. After months of preparation in the spring of 12 BC the offensive was launched. Drusus led his expeditionary force of seven legions in a series of annual campaigns – including an amphibious landing in the Ems estuary – moving eastwards from the Frisian coast towards the River Elbe (*Albis*). Only the accidental death of the commander in late 9 BC prematurely ended what had been a successful campaign.

His brother Tiberius assumed the task of completing the war. Between 8 and 7 BC he led expeditions, notably achieving the surrender of Maelo and forcible relocation of the Sugambri, but by then it was becoming evident that many of the free people of Germania would not kowtow. The Romans formed alliances with several nations, among them the Cherusci, and received hostages. Lucius Domitius Ahenobarbus – consul of 16 BC and grandfather of the future Emperor Nero – was the first Roman general to lead an army across the Elbe, in AD 1 or 2. As the first governor of the province Germania, he established its administrative capital at Ara Ubiorum (modern Cologne), the town constructed for the Ubii. At an altar dedicated to Rome and Augustus, delegates of the Germanic nations met in council to discuss matters affecting their communities under the aegis of a priest of German birth, Segimundus (AKA Segimund) of the Cherusci. War broke out again in AD 4 and 5 and Tiberius returned to squash the insurrection.

By AD 9 the province was undergoing a standard process of transformation. The legionaries began constructing a network of roads to connect military bases and laying out urban civilian settlements to host markets and courts to adjudicate in legal disputes. The aristocracies of the subject nations were being granted titles and limited powers of self-government within the Roman federal system and encouraged to resettle in towns. Having decision-making power (*imperium*) granted him by the emperor and with substantial military resources at his disposal, the then governor Publius Quinctilius Varus was responsible for driving the process of nation building, for ensuring internal security and protecting the interests of its Roman citizens. He was keen to see it through.

According to the most complete account to come down to us, the process of transforming the territory into a province before Varus became governor was proceeding at its own pace. The Germanic nations were adapting gradually to the changes being introduced by the Roman authorities. When Varus took office, however, that policy changed. 'In the discharge of his official duties,' writes Cassius Dio, Varus 'was administering the affairs of these peoples also, he strove to change them more rapidly. Besides issuing orders to them as if they were actually slaves of the Romans, he exacted money as he would from subject nations' (*Roman History* 56.18.3). He continues, 'To this they were in no mood to submit, for the leaders longed for their former ascendancy and the masses preferred their accustomed condition to foreign domination' (*Roman History* 56.18.4). Even so, the Germanic nations remained a disunited force. With roughly 30,000 legionaries and large numbers of *auxilia* deployed across the region, individually the German nations could not oust the Romans. To rally the anti-Roman sentiment the Germans needed to unite behind a single leader with a plan. According to Cassius Dio the German attack on the army of Quinctilius Varus was the vision of Arminius and his father Segimerus (AKA Segimer) of the Cherusci nation.

Segimerus had entered into a treaty with the Romans and had handed over his sons as hostages. Both were repatriated to Rome, where they learned Latin and Roman ways. Admitted as Roman citizens into the Equestrian Order, when old enough they became soldiers in the service of Rome, probably as *praefecti* of ethnic Cherusci cavalry. Velleius Paterculus states that Arminius 'had been associated with us constantly on private campaigns' (*Roman History* 2.118.2) which some interpret to mean the Great Illyrian Revolt (AD 6–9) in the western Balkans.

What pricked Arminius' conscience, turning him from a man enjoying the privileges of Roman civilization to a German patriot, is not preserved in the extant accounts. At some point he realized *he* should lead a national revolt, using his knowledge of Roman warcraft against them. How far in

This silver *denarius* minted in about 10 or 9 BC depicts a barbarian adult handing over a child into the care of Augustus who is seated on a curule chair. Exchanging hostages between enemies was a common practice in both Germanic and Roman societies. After surrendering to Tiberius in 7 BC chief Segimerus of the Cherusci handed over his sons Arminius and Flavus to the Roman commander. They were educated in Rome, raised as members of the Equestrian Order and trained to lead ethnic units of infantry, cavalry or both. (Kenneth J. Harvey. Author's collection)

The Roman province of Germania extended from the Rhine as far west as the Wadden Sea and as far east as the Elbe. It was the product of two decades of concerted military campaigns, beginning with Nero Claudius Drusus Germanicus (12–9 BC), continuing with his brother Tiberius Caesar (8–7 BC, AD 4–5) and concluding with Lucius Domitius Ahenobarbus (1 BC–AD 2), who resettled the Hermunduri and, having 'crossed the Elbe, meeting with no opposition, had made a friendly alliance with the barbarians on the further side' (Dio, *Roman History* 55.10a.2). He also moved the province's administrative centre from Vetera (Xanten) to Ara Ubiorum (Cologne).

Publius Quinctilius Varus was appointed as *legatus Augusti pro praetore* of Germania in AD 6 to promote the process of assimilation of the nations within its boundaries. Under his command were five legions and an unknown number of auxiliary cohorts and *alae*. The Roman army had moved successively from its original winter quarters of 12 BC on the Rhine to new bases along the courses of the Lippe (*Lupia*) and Main (*Moënus*) rivers. Its effort had shifted from war fighting to peace making, and was constructing a network of roads to connect the camps with stations and watch towers distributed across the newly occupied territories at the Germans' request, according to Dio. He also mentions civilian centres in Germania at this time, one of which – Waldgirmes in the Lahn Valley – has been identified, and others may yet remain to be discovered.

Assisting in the process were pro-Roman allies, among them the Angrivarii, Batavi, Cananefates, Chauci, Cherusci, Cugerni (the forcibly relocated Sugambri) and Frisii. As part of their treaty obligations, these *nationes* provided men and matériel for the Roman army. Though tipped off to expect trouble at the end of the summer of AD 9, Varus was unwilling to believe the Germanic peoples were going to rise in revolt. Arminius had assembled a formidable coalition of Angrivarii, Bructeri, Chatti, Chauci and Marsi to join his own Cherusci. Having signed a treaty with Tiberius in AD 6 the Marcomanni refused to join him.

advance the preparations for the uprising were made is not known. Arminius, meanwhile, had to convince his own people and others to rally behind him. Paterculus writes, 'At first, then, he admitted but a few, later a large number, to a share in his design; he told them, and convinced them too, that the Romans could be crushed, added execution to resolve, and named a day for carrying out the plot' (*Roman History* 2.118.3).

In his favour, Arminius enjoyed the complete trust of the governor. Key to the success of the revolt was to create a deception so convincing that Varus would believe it and not suspect his Cheruscan officer of treachery, then follow him on an unfamiliar route, whereupon his army would be ambushed. He knew that the Roman army would need to return to its winter camps at the end of the season, and that the legions were most vulnerable on the march. To reduce their numbers, the Germanic communities asked for Roman troops to be billeted with them, ostensibly to provide security and intervene in disputes.

The trap was set for a day in the late summer of AD 9. There was a tense moment when the plot was exposed. A noble of the Cherusci, Segestes, had learned of a deception planned by Arminius and Segimerus, and had gone straight to the governor. He disclosed everything he knew and demanded that the conspirators be arrested and clapped in chains. To his great surprise Varus not only refused to believe the informant 'but actually rebuked him for being needlessly excited and slandering his friends' (Cassius Dio, *Roman History* 56.19.3). In the weeks before the assault the father-and-son team had gone to great lengths to ingratiate themselves with Varus. They arranged to be close to him at all times and had shared meals with him, reassuring him that they would do everything demanded of them. They were the model barbarians. Their ploy worked. Varus' refusal to believe the tip-off from a credible source reassured the schemers and prompted them to move ahead with their plan.

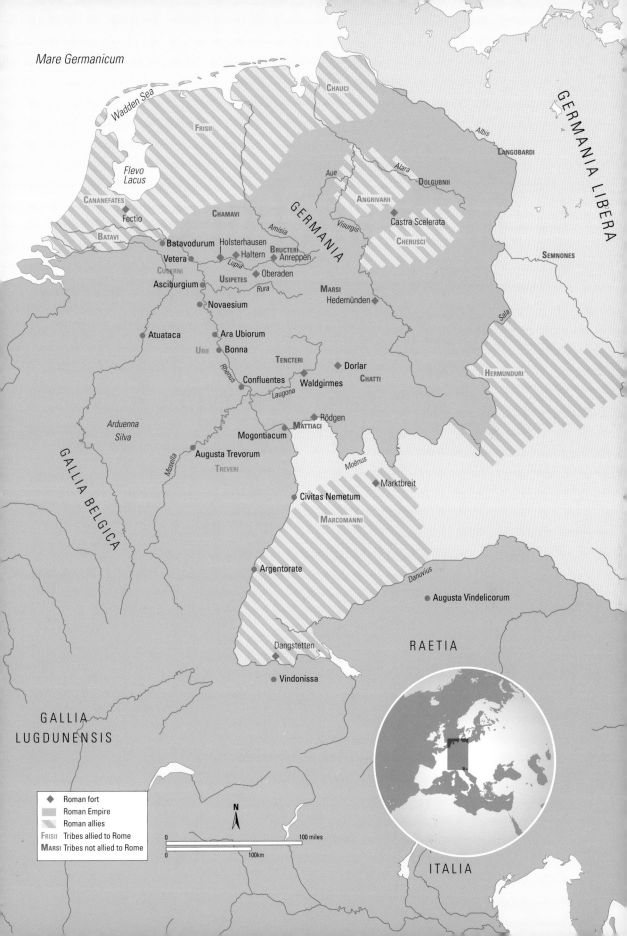

Mare Germanicum

Wadden Sea

GERMANIA LIBERA

FRISII

CHAUCI

Albis

LANGOBARDI

Flevo Lacus

Aue

Alara

ANGRIVARII

DOLGUBNII

CANANEFATES

Fectio

CHAMAVI

Amisia

GERMANIA

Visurgis

Castra Scelerata

SEMNONES

BATAVI

Batavodurum

Holsterhausen

Haltern

BRUCTERI

Anreppen

CHERUSCI

Vetera

Lupia

CUGERNI

Oberaden

USIPETES

Rura

MARSI

Asciburgium

Hedemünden

Sala

Novaesium

Atuataca

Ara Ubiorum

UBII

Bonna

TENCTERI

Dorlar

HERMUNDURI

Rhenus

Confluentes

Waldgirmes

CHATTI

Laugona

Arduenna Silva

Rödgen

MATTIACI

Mogontiacum

GALLIA BELGICA

Mosella

Augusta Trevorum

TREVERI

Moenus

Civitas Nemetum

Marktbreit

MARCOMANNI

Argentorate

Danuvius

Augusta Vindelicorum

RAETIA

Dangstetten

GALLIA LUGDUNENSIS

Vindonissa

ITALIA

Roman fort
Roman Empire
Roman allies
FRISII Tribes allied to Rome
MARSI Tribes not allied to Rome

N

0   100 miles
0   100km

The Opposing Sides

RECRUITMENT AND MOTIVATION

German

Germanic and Roman societies both highly valued the warrior ethos. Though there were stark differences between these ancient cultures, there were also striking similarities.

War fighting was a defining characteristic of most Germanic cultures. Demonstrating an aptitude for combat was a rite of passage for a boy. When he came of age, a young man was formally presented with his own lance and shield in the presence of his tribal assembly, a ritual regarded as the youth's admission to the public life of his community. In wartime, 100 of the ablest young men were selected from the nation's villages to accompany the cavalry on foot. Those able to run fast formed the vanguard of the attack because they were able to keep pace with the men on horseback. A select few, having proved their courage and skill, might then become retainers or companions of the clan or war chief. The Roman historian Cornelius Tacitus observes,

> there is an eager rivalry between the retainers for the post of honour next to their chief, as well as between different chiefs for the honour of having the most numerous and most valiant bodyguard. Here lie dignity and strength. To be perpetually surrounded by a large train of picked young warriors is a distinction in peace and a protection in war. (Tacitus, *Germania* 13)

As well as for the honour of serving the highest status man in the community, a warrior also fought for the prestige of his family. In battle the Germanic soldier formed up next to his kith and kin – son, brother, father and uncle, all stood side by side. Their lives depended on the men next to them, each looking out for the other. Often their wives and children would accompany them and cheer their menfolk from behind. 'Each man', writes Tacitus, 'feels bound to play the hero before such witnesses and to earn their most coveted praise. To his mother and to his wife he brings his wounds; and they do not shrink from counting them, nor from searching for them, while they carry food to the fighters and give them encouragement' (Tacitus, *Germania* 7).

When their man fell, his comrades and family would be there to carry home the body proudly upon his shield. For a warrior to run away and leave his shield behind was considered an act of shame and one that dishonoured him before his entire community. The punishment was exclusion from religious rites and denial of participation in the tribal assembly, and so great was the fear of this rejection that 'many such survivors from the battlefield have been known to end their shame by hanging themselves' (Tacitus, *Germania* 6).

Roman

Service with the Army was one of the very few formal careers open to a freeborn Roman citizen. It was a profession that paid a regular salary, provided opportunities for promotion and offered bonuses on special occasions, as well as the promise of booty from conquest and a cash payout for a life in retirement. The ranks of Rome's legions in the early 1st century AD were filled with volunteers (*volones*) who had to be at least 17 years of age. The sons of retired veteran soldiers living in the colonies as well as boys from the free cities and villages of Italy produced more than 61 per cent of the men serving with the eagles at that time. Before enrolment a young man had to pass an examination (*probatio*). Recruiters only picked men who were in good health and in good standing as Roman citizens. If he was married, enrolment was an automatic form of divorce. Once accepted he was given an indelible military mark and assigned to his legion.

After AD 6, when Caesar Augustus made reforms to pay and conditions, a new recruit (*probatus*) signed up as a *miles gregarius* for a fixed term of 20 years' service, at the end of which he received a cash gratuity of 12,000 *sestertii*. However, he was on call as a reservist (*evocatus*) for a further five years. *Evocati* served in separate detachments under their own commander (*curator*). A soldier in the Praetorian Cohorts (*Cohortes Praetoriae*), however, served only 16 years and was paid an end-of-service gratuity of 20,000 *sestertii*.

Soldiers swore an oath (*sacramentum*) to the Roman state and its consuls, not its legion commander. Each legion had an eagle (*aquila*) and sub-unit standards (*signa*) imbued with religious significance and to lose them was a humiliation (*infamia*); servicemen went to great lengths to ensure they did

Life as a warrior started young in Germanic societies. Young boys played with swords, spears and shields. A rite of passage into manhood was to perform at a gathering of the community to demonstrate his skills with weapons in a ritual dance. He was then given his own lance and shield. In war, 100 of the best young warriors accompanied the cavalry, running alongside them on foot in the vanguard. Having proven their courage and aptitudes in battle, the most valiant might be chosen to join the ranks of the chief's band of retainers. These men swore loyalty to the chief and fought for him, receiving food, clothing, a share of the war spoils and the prestige of being associated with the highest status figure in the community. (Tony Austin/Project Germani)

To join the Roman Army a recruit had to be male and at least 17 years of age. Writing of the legionary of the Early Empire, Vegetius notes 'in choosing recruits regard should be given to their trade. Fishermen, fowlers, confectioners, weavers, and in general all whose professions more properly belong to women should, in my opinion, by no means be admitted into the service. On the contrary, smiths, carpenters, butchers, and huntsmen are the most proper to be taken into it' (*On Military Matters* 1.7). He noted that the height requirement for legionaries of the First Cohort was fixed at 6ft, or at least 5ft 10in. He urged recruiters in his own day to pick brawny young men who stood up straight and had broad shoulders, narrow waists and strong hands with long fingers. The new recruit then went through a rigorous fitness and weapons-training programme. (The Ermine Street Guard)

not fall into enemy hands. Acts of valour by both individuals and entire units were publicly recognized with awards and titles. These could also be stripped for cowardice or under performance, as in the case of *Legio* I when Marcus Agrippa removed its honorary *Augusta* in the war in Spain of 19 BC. In the thick of battle, soldiers – then as now – were devoted to their comrades, to whom they referred as brothers (*fratres*) and for whose safety they constantly looked out.

Discipline (*disciplina*) was central to the *modus operandi* of the Roman Army. Disobedience and insubordination were severely punished. Sentries sleeping while on night duty could be punished by *fustuarium*, where the offender would be beaten with sticks by his comrades (*comilitiones*). Nevertheless corruption was endemic. By bribing a centurion or one of his staff, a soldier could buy time off or be switched to less arduous duties.

MORALE AND LOGISTICS

German

The relationship between the professional retainer and his chief was based on a combination of loyalty and honour, reward and recognition for services rendered:

> Upon the field of battle the chief is bound in honour not to let himself be surpassed in valour, and his retainers are equally bound to rival the valour of their chief. Furthermore, for one of the retainers to come back alive from the field where his chief had fallen is from that day forward an infamy and a reproach during all the rest of his life. To defend him, to guard him, nay, to give him the glory of their own feats of valour, is the perfection of their loyalty. The chiefs fight for victory; the bodyguard for their chief. (Tacitus, *Germania* 14)

A chieftain needed to wage war regularly to keep his retainers in peak condition and completely loyal. This helps explain the Germanic predisposition for what seem to have been unprovoked cross-border raids.

Not all members agreed with the tribal assembly's decisions or positions. Political factions and infighting were an inevitable part of tribal life. In signing a peace treaty with the Romans, Segimerus, the leader of the Cherusci, agreed to hand over his sons Arminius and Flavus as hostages. While both were well treated in captivity, nevertheless it seems he was later amenable to anti-Roman sentiments – similarly Arminius' uncle Inguiomerus – in contrast to the Cheruscan noble Segestes, who remained staunchly pro-Roman.

The elite warrior class was supplied with food and equipment by its chief, but the rank-and-file soldiers who were called upon to serve in wartime were also the farmers. When they left the fields to fight they relied upon their womenfolk and slaves to cultivate their crops and husband their herds. An over-extended fighting season could jeopardize the welfare of a community. Probably for this reason, after Arbalo (11 BC), as the Romans marched through their territory the Sugambri did little more than harry them. Weary and wounded from their inconclusive war with the Chatti, the Sugambri needed to return to their farms to bring in the summer's harvest before it was too late. To do otherwise might have meant starvation through the winter.

For a warrior to flee the battlefield or to surrender was considered an act of shame. This silver coin minted by moneyer Lucius Caninius Gallus in Rome c. 12 BC depicts a German surrendering his flag standard. While the figure represents a Roman stereotype of a barbarian in his nakedness, the die maker has faithfully preserved the long, swept-back hair and pointed beard, and the tasselled cloak beloved of Germanic warriors. (Michael V. Craton. Author's collection)

Roman

By AD 9, the focus of the Roman Army of the Rhine had shifted from conquest to pacification. War fighting was no longer its primary mission. Building roads and bridges and enforcing law and order were its priorities. The surveying instrument (*groma*) rather than the sword (*gladius*) was the tool used to spread its urban civilization. Roads were essential for moving men and matériel. A legionary's hobnailed boots often slipped on the rocky ground or grass when wet. When a Roman soldier was laden down with 60lb or more of armour and equipment on his shoulders, the uneven floor of a forest made marching exhausting work. It would have been particularly problematic for the wheeled carts (*vehicula*) that hauled the supplies required to provision the army. On campaign a legion would only carry enough food for about 15 days as it was expected to forage from the local surroundings to supplement and replenish its supplies. Now that Germania Magna was being pacified, however, foraging was no longer an option and the Roman Army would be expected to purchase from local traders any goods it could not obtain through the official supply chain co-ordinated by the military districts' commissariats in Mogontiacum (now Mainz) and Vetera (now Xanten).

While animals could feed off the land to some extent, large quantities of fodder nevertheless had to be provided. One estimate is that an *ala* with 560 horses required between 1,235lb and 3,705lb of barley, as well as 12,350lb of hay, each year. Carrying this volume by wagon or pack animal was impractical. To haul goods overland the Roman Army relied on vehicles with iron-rimmed wheels: the two-wheeled wagon pulled by oxen (*plaustrum*), the two-wheeled cart pulled by mules and the four-wheeled mule-driven wagon (both termed *carrus*). Mules were also used to carry bulky *contubernium* tents made of goatskin and stakes (*sudes*) to free legionaries from the burden. A *carrus* could carry between 950 and 1,435lb of supplies compared to more than 34 tons

The Roman Army – like its modern equivalent – marched on its stomach. The legion relied on a robust supply chain to provision it while on campaign. From the fortresses along the Rhine cargoes of heavy equipment and grain could be taken into Germania along the Ems (*Amisia*), Lippe and Main rivers by tubby barge as shown here in a scene from Trajan's Column, Rome. Stored in supply dumps, such as at Bentumersiel in Lower Saxony, foodstuffs and matériel could be moved overland by pack animal or wagon to their final point of consumption. (Conrad Cichorius, 1896)

in a small flat-bottomed barge measuring 65–112ft long and 10–15ft wide. For this reason the River Lippe (*Lupia*) was a critical link in the supply chain of Rome's pacification of Germania Magna, connecting the camps along the Rhine to supply dumps and forts in the newly occupied territories.

Civilian settlements quickly established themselves around military camps. There, traders (*lixae*) offered a wide range of goods and personal services, from food and drink, to special crafts and prostitution. The discovery of a Roman town at Waldgirmes east of the Rhine, complete with a *basilica* and a *forum* graced by a gold-plated bronze equestrian statue – probably of Caesar Augustus – the horse's head of which was found in 2009, indicates a growing confidence by Roman authorities that at least part of Germania was stable enough for urban development. Founded in 4 BC, it may have been an entrepôt where native Germanic producers could trade with Roman merchants and consumers. While the pottery fragments found were predominantly Roman, some 20 per cent of the ceramics were made by local Germanic craftsmen. The remains of other similar cities founded under Varus' governorship (mentioned in Cassius Dio, *Roman History* 56.18.2) may yet be found.

The pivot change from war fighting to peace making was not to all soldiers' liking. Men expected to augment their pay with war spoils and the peace dividend provided a meagre return for a soldier. Away from their permanent winter camps, the Roman soldiers found that the comforts afforded by marching camps were few. Centurions continued to enforce discipline, often harshly, meting out casual corporal punishment with their vine stick or assigning hard or unpleasant duties, such as latrine cleaning, for minor misdemeanours. Unless carefully managed, morale could sink and resentments grow.

TRAINING, DOCTRINE AND TACTICS

German

A young warrior spent his days in training. From the earliest age he was exposed to the warrior ethos and learned to use the iron-tipped lance (*framea*) – which could be thrust, swung and thrown – and brightly painted wooden shield with its iron boss. Demonstrating skill in the use of weapons was a cause for celebration. At gatherings of the tribe, 'Naked youths who practise the sport bound in the dance amid swords and lances that threaten their lives. Experience gives them skill, and skill again gives grace; profit or pay are out of the question; however reckless their pastime, its reward is the pleasure of the spectators' (Tacitus, *Germania* 24).

As a professional retainer the warrior had to be fed and kept usefully employed: 'Forays and plunderings supply the means of keeping a free table' (Tacitus, *Germania* 14). In the eyes of the Roman elite, that meant the Germanic warrior was a *latro*, a bandit, and his unlawful excursion into Roman territory was criminal banditry (*latronicum*). 'Robberies which are committed beyond the boundaries of each state', wrote Caesar, 'bear no infamy [to them] and they avow that these are committed for the purpose of disciplining their youth and of preventing sloth' (Caesar, *Gallic War* 6.23).

Before engaging their enemy Germanic warriors fired up their spirits by singing and chanting. According to Tacitus the German war fighter and his fellows sang to Hercules (whom the historian may have equated to Thor or Irmin, son of Wuotan):

> They raise a hymn in his praise, as the pattern of all valiant men, as they approach the field of battle. They have also a kind of song which they chant to fire their courage – they call it 'barding' [*barritus*] – and from this chant they draw an augury of the issue of the coming day. For they inspire terror in the foe, or become flurried themselves according to the sound that goes up from the host. It is not so much any articulate expression of words as a war-like chorus. Their great aim is to produce a hoarse and tempestuous roar, every man holding his shield before his mouth to increase the volume and depth of tone by reverberation. (Tacitus, *Germania* 3)

Augmenting the raucous noise, the men struck their weapons rhythmically against their shields. Some worked themselves into a frenzy through the medium of dance to antagonize and strike fear into their opponent.

The 'hit-and-run' ambush was the preferred tactic, leveraging the element of surprise to strike the enemy when he was least expecting an attack. They were particularly successful against Roman troops on route marches, as Drusus the Elder discovered in 11 BC. At Arbalo his army was blockaded in a narrow pass by the Germans. It appears the decision by the Cheruscan leadership not to press home their advantage allowed the Roman commander and his men to escape.

Co-ordinated campaigns and set-piece battles were also fought. One is recorded – the year is unspecified – by an alliance of Angrivarii and Chamavi who set upon the Bructeri. The alliance 'entered their settlements, drove them out and utterly exterminated them with the common help of the neighbouring tribes, either from hatred of their tyranny, or from the attractions of plunder, or from Heaven's favourable regard for us [the Romans] ... More than 60,000 fell' (Tacitus, *Germania* 33). Other tribes were also capable of assembling in

While many Germanic societies were ruled by kings, others elected a leader in wartime, chosen for his prowess. He was granted power of life and death over the men in his charge for the period he held the position. This war chief depicted here wears a mail shirt of iron links over a woollen tunic and trousers. An iron sword hangs in its scabbard from a baldric. A fine leather belt completes his panoply. He is also equipped with two lances – a long *framea* and a short spear. His shield is the long hexagonal type often depicted on Roman coins and friezes. (Tony Austin/Project Germani)

COMBAT

1

3

6

This artwork depicts a retainer of the Cherusci nation, a Germanic tribe that fought at Teutoburg Pass, Weser River, Idistaviso and the Angrivarian Wall under its war chief Arminius. The retainers of the tribal chief were full-time combat soldiers fighting for a share of war spoils, status and bragging rights. During his early adult life this man would have fought in raids against neighbouring tribes. When chief Segimerus agreed that the Cherusci should became allies of the Romans in 7 BC, that warrior lifestyle changed and he reluctantly had to turn his hand to farming and trade. When war broke out he willingly fought the Romans again, in AD 4 and 5. Four years later, now in his early 30s, he is shown here as he charges towards the enemy, wielding the lance he has trained to use since childhood.

Weapons, dress and equipment

This man is perfectly equipped for the Germanic landscape of open fields, forests and swamps. The weapons available to a high-status Germanic warrior included the long lance (*framea*; **1**) with an iron blade at the tip. Made in a range of lengths it could be swung, thrust or thrown at an opponent. Swords were less common. A long, double-edged iron sword was used to thrust and stab, while a single-edged weapon (**2**) was used like a cleaver to chop and cut. A flat shield (**3**) made of wooden planks could be faced with leather or left bare and was painted with a blazon. The domed iron shield boss protected the single hand grip at the rear.

This warrior would have always grown his hair long but for this battle has tied it up in a figure of eight or 'Suebian' knot without using a fastener. (It is described by Tacitus (*Germania* 38) and an example of it survives with the Osterby Man whose decapitated head (dated to between AD 1 and 100) was found in 1948 at Kohlmoor, a peat bog near Osterby, Germany.) He moves quickly on simple leather shoes (**4**) that could be easily repaired or replaced. Germanic warriors travelled light, generally eschewing bulky – and noisy – protective head and body gear, which was expensive to manufacture and difficult to repair, especially if foreign in origin. The soldier of Ancient Germany went to war in textiles. Loose fitting woollen trousers or leather breeches with leg bindings were standard attire (**5**). From a decorated leather belt around the waist hung personal hygiene items and a scabbard for an iron knife (**6**). Wearing a long-sleeved tunic (**7**) was optional and, indeed, many fought bare-chested. Cloaks (**8**) in bright colours and bold patterns, pinned at the shoulder with a brooch, were a source of pride and often worn in battle.

Germanic warriors assembled in columns or rows with spaces between them for manoeuvrability and formed up to face the enemy in dense lines or wedge formations. Here, the shield wall and the general charge are depicted. The men in each row interleaved or overlapped their shields to form a shield wall or 'shield castle'. The retainers – elite, professional warriors called 'the Hundred' – stood in rows, here shown three men deep; lower-class tribesmen stood behind them, but in no particular order, ready to charge. The formation could push forward aggressively into their opponents' ranks using clubs, *frameae* and swords at close quarters. The infantry might operate in tandem with cavalry. 'On the whole, one would say that their chief strength is in their infantry, which fights along with the cavalry; admirably adapted to the action of the latter is the swiftness of certain foot-soldiers, who are picked from the entire youth of their country, and stationed in front of the line' (Tacitus, *Germania* 6).

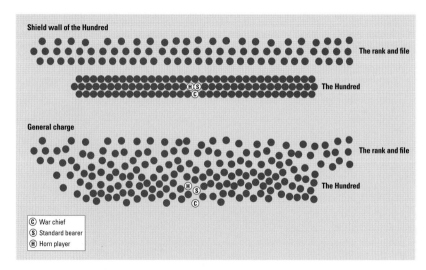

Shield wall of the Hundred

The rank and file

The Hundred

General charge

The rank and file

The Hundred

Ⓒ War chief
Ⓢ Standard bearer
Ⓗ Horn player

OPPOSITE
The Roman legionary was trained and equipped for set-piece battles in large formations and siege warfare as at the Angrivarian Wall. He fought best as a member of a tactical unit in a disciplined formation. Outside his preferred battleground of open plains and hillsides he was less well adapted, and relied on auxiliary troops in these circumstances, as at Weser River. (The Ermine Street Guard)

columns or rows and taking up wedge formations. The men in the wedge interleaved or overlapped their shields to form a shield wall or 'shield castle'. Iulius Caesar records how in 58 BC, the Germanic king, Ariovistus, arrayed his men against the Romans by assembling the seven tribes under his command in columns of 300 men strong with spaces between them to allow manoeuvrability. The Germanic left flank (as seen from the Roman side) – the side unprotected by the shield or handheld weapon – collapsed under the initial Roman attack, but on the right flank – the protected side – Ariovistus' men were able to deflect the Romans. They pushed forward aggressively into Caesar's own ranks. They might even have won had Roman reinforcements not arrived in time to save Caesar.

To the blast of trumpets a hail of spears, darts and rocks would be unleashed upon the enemy. From the front and centre the war chief led his men in a line or wedge charge. Racing out ahead screaming in a form of war madness, some young men (later called *berserkers*) – who carried shields and wielded spears or clubs, but were otherwise naked and barefoot – might throw themselves upon the enemy. During the ensuing mêlée, retreats and feigned flights intended to confuse or trick the opponent were accepted battlefield tactics.

Roman authors often portrayed the Germanic army on the battlefield as a rabble, but this is inaccurate. There were differences in battle strategies between tribes. In particular, Tacitus was struck by the similarities between the army of the Chatti and his own people's, from their reliance on infantry and their hierarchical command structure, to their use of formations and temporary camps with entrenchments. Thus in 11 BC when the Sugambri invaded the territory of the Chatti intent on a quick and decisive raid, they found themselves embroiled with an opponent more used to planned campaigns – and a long, drawn-out war ensued.

Roman

On arrival at his designated camp, the new recruit began a rigorous programme of basic training. There were trainers for each aspect of war fighting. Drill was

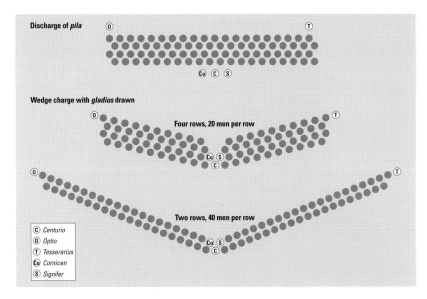

Discharge of *pila*

Wedge charge with *gladius* drawn

Four rows, 20 men per row

Two rows, 40 men per row

C *Centurio*
O *Optio*
T *Tesserarius*
Co *Cornicen*
S *Signifer*

Roman troops fought in battle lines (*acies*) – closed or open order – and in formation, such as the triangle or wedge (*cuneus*). Here, the normal line-up, in which *pila* would be thrown, is shown along with two variants of the wedge formation, used during the charge with swords drawn. According to one late Roman-period commentator on military matters, 'the soldiers call it the pig's head (*caput porcinum*)' (Vegetius 3.19). In a wedge the century of 80 legionaries re-aligned on either side of the centurion, dressing their line so that they formed two angled sides of an arrowhead. 'The wedge is a disposition of a body of infantry widening gradually towards the base and terminating in a point towards the front. It pierces the enemy's line by a multitude of darts directed to one particular place' (Vegetius 3.19). With their shields positioned to protect the full front of their bodies they unsheathed their *gladii* and held them ready to thrust as they plunged into the enemy line.

conducted under the critical eye and hoarse voice of the *campidoctor*. The novice legionary learned to march, run in full kit, jump, swim and to ride a horse if he did not already know how to do so. On the battlefield the legionary would need to respond instantly and unquestioningly to commands to take his designated place. Romans fought in battle lines (*acies*) – in closed or open order – and in formation – the wedge (*cuneus*) and tortoise (*testudo*). All required honed spatial-awareness skills, concentration and stamina.

Weapons training (*armatura*) was supervised by the *doctor armorum*. The recruit learned to throw the *pilum* – the legionary's trademark javelin, featuring a slender iron shank with a sharp pyramid-shaped point, attached by an iron collar, iron rivets and a wooden pin to a wooden shaft. If it struck the opponent's flesh the trauma could cause injury or death. If it pierced his protective wooden shield, the weight of the wooden shaft might bend the narrow iron shank or break it off at the collar so it could not be thrown back, rendering the opponent's equipment unusable. In battle the legionary would unleash one or two *pila* at a range of roughly 30ft from the enemy and then advance in a charge with sword drawn. To develop his technique in the use of the *gladius* and his arm strength, the novice started with a double-weighted wooden sword, eventually exchanging it for the real thing. During training the novice learned how to use the shield (*scutum*) with its domed iron boss (*umbo*) as a weapon to punch his opponent before stabbing with the *gladius*.

To build endurance and strength he went on long route marches. The Roman soldier was expected to march 20 Roman miles in half of a summer day, but 24 Roman miles at a fast military pace in the same time (Vegetius, *On Military Matters* 1.9). At the end of it, he would build a temporary camp, using the *groma* to lay out its streets, and the entrenching tool to dig the ditch and raise the rampart, upon which he placed the two stakes (*sudes*) assigned each man. Training was constant and unending. Some 60 years later, a former enemy of the Romans who had witnessed in awe the dedication of Roman troops to military exercises would write that 'their drills were bloodless battles, and their battles were bloody drills' (Josephus, *Jewish War* 3.70).

This artwork depicts a legionary of *Legio* XIX, which fought – and was wiped out – at Teutoburg Pass. Born in one of the Italian *coloniae*, aged 17 this man would have joined the legion as a volunteer at its winter camp on the Rhine, received his military mark, sworn an oath of loyalty and undergone extensive training. Since Tiberius Caesar's campaigns in AD 4 and 5 this legionary has seen little actual combat action in Germania. Now in his early 30s and still unmarried in accordance with Army regulations, he has spent his career largely occupied with pacification activities in the interior of the new province, such as patrolling and taking part in engineering construction works. He is seen here standing his ground ready to defend himself from a direct frontal attack.

Weapons, dress and equipment

This man is well equipped for the northern European theatre of war. Once the javelin (*pilum*) was launched, the soldier advanced with sword (*gladius*; **1**) drawn and shield (*scutum*) held close. The shield (**2**) was used for both defence and offence. The large size and curved shape covered the front of the soldier from chin to knee. The domed iron boss (**3**), which protected the left hand, was used to punch an opponent before lunging forward with the bayonet-like *gladius*. If the sword was lost, a short, leaf-shaped dagger (*pugio*; **4**) was the weapon of last resort – these were popular trade and war trophy items with Germanic tribesman.

The Roman soldier marched on stout leather boots (*caligae*; **5**). The open design let the feet breathe in summer, but they could be worn with woollen socks in winter. Iron hobnails protected the thick leather sole from wear and provided traction on the ground. The iron helmet (*galea*; **6**) – based on a Gallic design with Roman adaptations – encased the skull. The attached guard at the brow would take

blows from a spearpoint or sword to the front, while the wide, integral guard at the rear protected the neck. The large cheek plates were shaped for maximum protection without sacrificing visibility. The body armour (*lorica*; **7**) shown here was the state-of-the-art articulated, segmented plate design and is based on finds at the Kalkrieser Berg near Osnabrück in Germany. The curved iron plates attached to leather straps on the inside. The upper left and right shoulder assemblies attached to the left and right girdle assemblies by external leather straps with buckles. Worn over a woollen tunic (**8**), the armour allowed for full movement of the upper body and spread the 22lb weight evenly across the shoulders. A neckerchief (*focale*; **9**) prevented chafing. Suspended from the waist belt, a protective sporran (*cingulum*; **10**) of leather straps with metal plates protected the groin and genitals. The complete kit weighed between 25lb and 45lb, with pack equipment contributing an additional 30lb or so.

LEADERSHIP AND COMMUNICATIONS

German

In nations that did not have hereditary kings, to administer the law in the community a chieftain was elected by a tribal assembly. Each leader had a council of 100 free men, which he consulted for advice and through which he enforced his decisions. For a military campaign the community elected a war leader. Iulius Caesar observes 'when a state either repels war waged against it or wages it against another, magistrates are chosen to preside over that war with such authority, that they have power of life and death' (Caesar, *Gallic War* 6.23). When the campaign concluded, the war leader relinquished his power. 'They choose their kings for their noble birth,' remarks Tacitus, 'their commanders for their prowess: the king's power is neither unlimited nor arbitrary, and the generals owe their authority less to their military rank than to their example and the admiration they excite by it, if they are dashing, if they are conspicuous, if they charge ahead of the line' (Tacitus, *Germania* 7).

On the battlefield, warriors gathered around a battle standard designed like the *vexillum* of the Roman Army. The clan flag was a prized totem and surviving Roman coins display them as a war spoil or being handed over in an act of surrender by a defeated warrior. The Germans respected an opponent who had fought well but lost. A live enemy captive might expect to face a duel with the champion of the captor's tribe. The combat was accepted as a means of divination and its outcome believed to be a prognosis of how the war would finally end.

Little is known about battlefield communications and intelligence-gathering practices among the Germanic tribes. Capabilities and needs would have differed according to the circumstances of each nation. Some appear to have been settled in one location, living in scattered farmsteads or hamlets, while others migrated, invading the settled rural communities and often displacing them. News of incursions across disputed borders must have been relayed to tribal seniors, even if only to appeal for help. The Cherusci observed the Romans at a distance from the cover of forest before launching their ambushes. The failure of the Sugambri to gather and use intelligence to understand the Chatti might also help explain why they found themselves embroiled in a long campaign when they had only prepared for a punitive raid.

Roman

A legionary's primary loyalty was to his century (*centuria*), the basic fighting unit of the Roman Army, comprised of

80 men, not 100. It consisted of ten 'tent parties' (*contubernia*). The eight men in a *contubernium* shared a tent and soldiers often referred to themselves as *contubernales*, the equivalent of 'messmates'. Six such centuries constituted a *cohors* of 480 men. There were nine cohorts of this size in a legion, but the First Cohort was double-strength and brought the full roster of active troops to 5,280.

The officer in charge of the century was a *centurio*, who carried a vine staff (*vitis*) with which to administer casual corporal punishment. He was a tough, battle-hardened officer who had worked his way through the ranks. A man of reasonable literacy and with a clean service record might aspire to the centurionate after 15–20 years of military service. Each cohort had a tiered centurionate whose titles recalled the tripartite ranks of the old citizen army from the days of the Republic. The most senior was the *centurio pilum prior*, followed by the *princeps prior* and the *hastatus prior*, then the *centurio pilum posterior*, *princeps posterior* and *hastatus posterior*. Those men below the rank of *centurio* but above the common soldiery were designated *principales*. They enjoyed better rates of pay than the regular troops and shared the *centurio*'s quarters. Also billeted with the centuries were mounted legionaries – 120 in all – of the elite *equites legionis*, who performed duties as escorts and messengers.

Occupying the next rank up in the command structure were five junior officers from the Order of Knights (*ordo equester*) called *tribuni angusticlavii*, 'narrow stripe' tribunes, who acted as advisors to the legion commander or attended to his administrative needs. These five oversaw physical training, managed the granaries and hospital, supervised security at the camp gates and enforced the law. They were aged in their late teens or early twenties; this was their first term of military service as they sought to move up the political career ladder (*cursus honorum*).

Third in seniority was the *praefectus castrorum*, holder of a new rank just introduced under Augustus, and one which can be considered a true army career position. This officer was responsible for the operational aspects of the camp – the structural integrity of the installations including the ramparts, sanitation and the hospital, as well as the supervision of the drill and weapons trainers and upkeep of the artillery. As the artillery was under his command, he directed operations during a siege. While the legion was on the march, the *praefectus* was responsible for the baggage train (*impedimenta*). Second in command of a legion was a *tribunus laticlavius*, named after the broad purple stripe on his senatorial toga. Each man in this

On the battlefield, Roman commanders used a variety of methods to communicate with men in each *centuria*. Each century of the Roman Army employed a cornet player (*cornicen*) who played a curved bronze horn (*cornu*). The *cornu* provided an aural means to relay orders, such as to fall in, march, charge, regroup or retreat. It would be used in conjunction with the standard (*signum*), which provided visual confirmation of the order. Vegetius writes 'the *cornicenes* are used only to regulate the motions of the *signa* … The *cornicenes* sound whenever the *signa* are to be struck or planted' (*On Military Matters*, 2.22). A skilled musician can sound a range of notes with this instrument. In the thick of battle orders could be communicated above the din of formation changes and close-quarters combat. (The Ermine Street Guard)

position would be rotated out quickly as his next career position was to serve as a *quaestor* back in Rome or in one of the provinces; later in his career he might return to the Army as commander of his own legion. In overall command of these 6,000 men was the *legatus legionis*. Hand-picked by Augustus, this man was his deputy (*legatus*) who held delegated military power (*imperium*). In his forties or fifties, he served a term of three to four years with any given legion. As a member of the senatorial class, he was usually educated and well connected socially.

The Roman army commander made extensive use of strategic and tactical military intelligence, though whether it was systematic – in the modern sense that it was processed, assessed and disseminated by a formal organization – is not clear. Methods such as diplomacy, espionage and monitoring news flow – at military installations and civilian locations such as markets – were employed to identify trouble spots or plan specific actions. Useful information could also be gathered by interviewing friendly allies informally, though hostile captives could be interrogated – often under torture – by specialist troops (*speculatores*). On the march, typically between 7 and 28 miles – or up to three hours' ride – ahead of the main column, scouts (*exploratores*) carried out reconnaissance duties (*exploratio*). They would ride back to the commander periodically with reports of activity or conditions. It was for the commander to determine if he should act on the information – or not act, as in the case of Varus in AD 9. Iulius Caesar was a keen practitioner of

intelligence gathering and his *Commentaries on the Gallic War* are full of examples of his use of it.

USE OF ALLIES AND AUXILIARIES

German

Much as the nations of Germania Magna were fiercely jealous of their independence, they were, nevertheless, able and willing to co-operate and form alliances to achieve a common goal. Smaller warrior bands would sometimes come together to form coalitions, such as the migrant Suebi or Suevi – the oldest of whom were reportedly the Semnones – and their neighbours the Langobardi, Hermunduri and Marcomanni.

One attractive target was raiding for Roman loot. In the absence of a written treaty, to bind each party the partners might carry out a trial raid upon the agreed enemy to demonstrate their commitment to the project. Of the raid in 17 BC Florus writes, 'The three powerful nations of the Cherusci, Suebi and Sugambri, had commenced the war by burning twenty of our centurions, regarding this proceeding as a bond of union, and entertaining such confident hopes of victory, that they divided the spoil by agreement beforehand' (Florus, *Epitome* 2.30.24). The Cherusci chose the horses, the Suebi the gold and silver and the Sugambri the human captives. It was the Sugambri 'who live near the Rhenus, that began the war' under their war chief Maelo (Strabo, *Geography* 7.1.4). The Chatti were approached by emissaries of the Sugambri, but refused to take part. Another cause for an alliance was the loss of territory to another tribe, in the hope that new land could be taken. In the raid across the Rhine the Sugambri were also joined by their neighbours, the Tencteri and Usipetes. They had been looking for new homelands during Iulius Caesar's Gallic War (58–50 BC), having lost their native country to the Suebi who had encroached south-westwards from the Elbe.

It was common practice for the war-chiefs of the alliance to exchange hostages – often members of their own families – as bonds of good faith. Yet that trade might not be enough to guarantee trust. Alliances could be transient. Strabo observed that at different times one nation would grow powerful, strike out at its neighbours, then sue for peace, exchange hostages, grow restless and rebel, in so doing betraying both their word and the 'human shields' they had handed over. During the second year of Drusus the Elder's German Wars, the Sugambri raided the territory of the Chatti in response to the latter's refusal to join them in 17 BC. Yet a year later they were fighting on the same side against the legions of the Roman invader.

At different times the Germanic nations saw the Romans as allies. Among them were the Batavi, Cananefates, Chauci, Cherusci, Frisii and Ubii. As part of their treaty obligations, they provided troops and supplies for the Roman Army. On account of their tall stature and 'barbaric' appearance, Germanic soldiers were regarded with awe by urban Romans.

Augustus had a personal paramilitary force that acted as his bodyguard independently of the Praetorian Cohorts. The *Germani Corporis Custodes* were recruited from the Batavi and Ubii and organized into one or more units of 30 men (*decuria*), each commanded by a *decurio* and his *optio*.

Roman

As Rome's influence spread during the years of the Republic, the Romans signed treaties with the city-states and nations they encountered. The terms of these treaties obliged both parties to come to the assistance of the other when called upon in wartime, or at least to remain neutral in a conflict with a third party. In this way the Romans augmented their own forces on campaign with legions recruited from their allies (*socii, foederati*). After the Social War of 91–88 BC the Italians joined the regular Roman legions, but non-Italians continued to serve as auxiliary – or 'helper' – troops (*auxilia*). The *Cohors* II *Tungrorum*, for example, was recruited from among men of the Tungri nation living near the Arduenna Silva (Ardennes Forest) of Gallia Belgica. Iulius Caesar made extensive use of *auxilia* on campaign in both the Gallic War and the Civil War (49–45 BC). Auxiliaries continued in the service of Rome as a permanent part of the Army under Augustus and Tiberius. They provided a variety of specialist fighting skills, such as Cretan archers (*sagittarii*) with powerful composite bows and irregular troops from the Balearic Islands using deadly accurate slings (*funditores*) to throw slingshot (*glandes*). Auxiliaries served for 25 years and on honourable completion of service were granted Roman citizenship, which could be passed on to their children – who, in turn, might enrol with the legions.

At the turn of the 1st century BC/AD the auxiliary infantryman's basic equipment – helmet, body armour, shield – did not differ greatly from that of the legionary, but many a soldier from abroad would have brought with him much of his own panoply of arms – bows, shields, slings, spears and swords – that characterized his nationality and suited his mode of combat.

Auxiliary infantry were organized into cohorts (*cohors peditata milliaria*) of 800 – not a thousand men – each sub-divided into ten *centuriae* of 80 men like the regular legions. They were usually trained to the same high standards as legionaries and, like them, their centuries were led by centurions and *optiones* and they marched under their own *signa* carried by *signiferi*. Commanding the entire unit was a tribune (*tribunus cohortis*). Mixed units (*cohors equitata quingenaria*), each comprising six *centuriae* of infantry and four *turmae* of cavalry for a total of 608 men, were commanded by a prefect (*praefectus cohortis*). They were often deployed for local garrison and police duties in imperial provinces, such as Germania. A unit of this kind recruited from among the Germanic Ubii nation is known from an inscription dating to Tiberius' reign.

Cavalry from Batavia, Gaul and the Rhineland were particularly valued for their skills in horsemanship. These were often deployed as advance skirmishers (*procursatores*) or *exploratores* as well as shock troops. Auxiliary cavalry were organized into *alae* – literally 'wings' – of 512 or 768 men, sub-divided into 16 or 24 *turmae* respectively. An *ala* might be composed of men of a single nation fighting under its chief (*dux*), as Arminius of the Cherusci or Chariovalda of the Batavi, after whom the unit was named. A *turma* was commanded by a *decurio*, assisted by a *duplicarius*. Details of which auxiliary units were assigned to Varus' and Germanicus' command are not preserved in the extant records, but it is certain they were a key part of the Romans' provincial army.

The Roman Army was made up of roughly equal numbers of citizen legionaries and alien auxiliaries. The non-Roman troops augmented the Roman forces with specialist skills, including archers, slingers and cavalry, using their own arms and equipment and styles of fighting, like these men on Trajan's Column. Ethnic cavalry *alae* or mixed *cohortes* of infantry and cavalry often served under their own native commanders (*duces*). At the end of 25 years they were granted Roman citizenship and their sons could enlist with the legions. (Conrad Cichorius, 1896)

Teutoburg Pass

Summer AD 9

BACKGROUND TO BATTLE

AD 9 had been a good year for the Romans. Varus' army had been able to move freely across the peaceful province of Germania, carrying out its now routine programme of police duties and road building. The *legatus Augusti pro praetore* had with him three *legiones*, three *alae* of cavalry and six *cohortes* of auxiliaries (Velleius Paterculus, *Roman History* 2.117.1). *Legiones* XIIX and XIX are known with certainty to have been part of his army group and XVII is presumed to have been the other since it is attested nowhere else. At full strength that would represent 22,752 men at arms, consisting of 16,800 legionaries including 360 mounted scouts, 3,072 cavalry (based on 512 men per *ala*) and 2,880 infantry auxiliaries (assuming 480 men per *cohors peditata*). In reality, however, the force was likely to be significantly smaller – perhaps as few as 14,000 men. Detachments of the provincial army would have remained at the winter camps – Batavodurum (now Nijmegen), Vetera, Novaesium (now Neuss), Ara Ubiorum and Mogontiacum – to ensure they were maintained and stocked with provisions, while others would have been seconded to the provincial administration running the legal and military affairs of Germania. Two legions – *Legiones* I and V *Alaudae* – had remained on the Rhine under the command of Varus' nephew, Lucius Nonius Asprenas. Additionally, at the start of the season some of the main force would have been declared unfit for duty on account of sickness (Romans soldiers frequently suffered ailments of the eyes) or recovering from wounds, and had to remain in camp to recuperate. Accompanying the troops was an unknown number of assorted non-combatants – slaves, merchants and personal-service providers (men, women and children) – who made a living from trading with the soldiers and local tribespeople they encountered.

The extant accounts do not indicate where Varus and his army had been during the spring and summer seasons. They may have marched from the Rhine to beyond the Weser into the territory of the Dolgubnii or as far as the Elbe, where Rome's most north-easterly allies – the Hermunduri – lived. Alternatively, they may have been in the territory of the Chauci in the north-west. One tantalizing clue is a temporary marching camp dating to this period – found in Porta Westfalica, near Minden, in 2008 – which could have been constructed by Varus' men on their outbound or inbound march. Some time in August or September, Varus gave the order for his legions to dismantle their summer camp and to begin the long trek south back to their winter quarters along the Lippe or Rhine rivers. To reach them Varus' army would have to traipse through the territories of several Germanic nations –

The legionary on the march was nicknamed 'Marius' mule' after the consul who required soldiers to carry much of their own equipment in order to reduce the length of the baggage train (*impedimenta*) and speed up troop movement. A legionary typically carried a change of clothing, three days' rations, a water bottle, a pan, a length of chain, entrenching tool and an axe, all suspended from a T-shaped pole borne over the shoulder; this could add another 30lb. Additionally, he carried two palisade stakes and two *pila*. (The Ermine Street Guard)

among them the Angrivarii, Cherusci, Bructeri and Marsi. Anticipating the route, Arminius successfully negotiated with the leadership of each tribe to join the conspiracy. In turn they agreed they would launch surprise attacks when the Romans were most vulnerable and inflict heavy casualties. It would be a war of steady attrition in which the army of occupation would ultimately be destroyed.

As far as the governor was concerned the province was at peace. Then Varus received a report of 'an uprising, first on the part of those who lived at a distance from him' (Cassius Dio, *Roman History* 56.19.3). It was the decoy. As the Roman column departed from the camp, Arminius rode up to Varus with a request that his *ala* be excused. He gave as his reason the need to ride ahead 'to assemble their allied forces' (Cassius Dio, *Roman History* 56.19.4). This would not have struck Varus as strange, as the auxiliaries were dispersed across the territory on various duties and would have to rejoin Arminius' unit to make the journey to their winter camp. The column continued on. This was uncharted territory and there was no road. The pioneers in the vanguard felled trees to clear a way forward and constructed simple bridges to cross those rivers too deep to traverse by foot. Late in the afternoon Varus despatched a rider to relay the message to the legate of the legion in the vanguard to find a suitable spot, deploy his men and establish a marching camp for the night. The legionaries dug a circumvallated space large enough for the three legions to erect their serried rows of *contubernium* tents, with Varus' mobile headquarters (*principia*) at the centre and accommodations for the mounted units on the periphery. As the evening drew in the last of the men entered the camp and set up their goatskin tents. While designated men slept, pickets were posted to patrol the parapet through the night.

MAP KEY

1 0800hrs (approx.), Day 1: Varus sets off in the direction of the winter camps on the Rhine with three legions, three *alae* and six cohorts of auxiliary troops, forming a convoy stretching over many miles.

2 Mid-morning (approx.), Day 1: Varus receives intelligence of an uprising ahead. Arminius approaches Varus requesting permission to take his men promising he will return with allies. Varus agrees. The Romans follow. They have to cut a way through the forest. Germanic alliance troops murder the Roman troops billeted at road stations and staging posts located in their communities.

3 Early evening, Day 1: The Romans erect their marching camp for the night.

4 Early morning, Day 2: The Romans march on. Troops, baggage and non-combatants are reported as mixed together and in no particular marching order.

5 Afternoon, Day 2: The Germans rain missiles down on the Roman line. The baggage carts block the way out. The Germans close in. The Romans take casualties but maintain unit cohesion. Wind and heavy rain hinder the Romans' escape.

6 Evening, Day 2: The Romans construct a marching camp on a wooded hill for the night. Varus orders all but essential baggage destroyed or abandoned.

7 Dawn, Day 3: Varus' men depart early to establish some distance between themselves and the insurgents and aim to reach Fort Aliso on the River Lippe. They exit the forest and cut across open country. The Roman column thins out.

8 Afternoon, Day 3: The Germans resume their attacks on the Roman line, breaking it into smaller groups, then surrounding and overwhelming them. The Romans enter forest again and come under the most sustained and heaviest attack so far. In the confined spaces between the trees the Roman infantry and cavalry get in each other's way and sustain casualties.

9 Evening, Day 3: The Romans establish a camp. Varus discusses the available options with his officers. Lucius Eggius proposes surrender.

10 Morning, Day 4: The wind and rain continue. The Germans continue to attack the Roman troops. Numonius Vala attempts to break out with cavalry.

11 Afternoon (approx.), Day 4: The Germans attack again. Varus commits suicide. His severed head is presented to Arminius, who sends it to Marboduus of the Marcomanni.

12 Evening (approx.), Day 4: The first escapees reach the Roman fort at Aliso and are received by the senior officer, Lucius Caecidius.

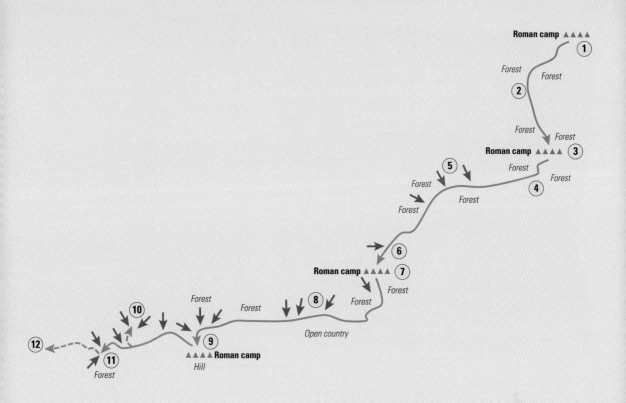

Battlefield environment

The ambush of the Roman army on the march over four days was spread over a corridor of land dozens of miles long. The early 1st-century AD Roman general turned historian Velleius Paterculus characterizes the environment of the battle-space as set among 'forests and marshes' (*Roman History* 2.119.2) – words also used by Florus (*Epitome* 2.30). The 3rd-century historian Cassius Dio – who gives us the most complete account of the events – describes mountains that 'had an uneven surface broken by ravines, and the trees grew close together and very high' (*Roman History* 56.20.1). Similarly he writes of the weather on the first day of the Germanic attacks 'a violent rain and wind came up that separated them still further, while the ground, that had become slippery around the roots and logs, made walking very treacherous for them, and the tops of the trees kept breaking off and falling down, causing much confusion' (*Roman History* 56.20.3). Both are Roman stereotypes of *barbaricum* in the north beyond the borders of the civilized world rather than accurate topographical and meteorological descriptions for the place and time of the battle.

Tacitus specifically calls the site of the Varian Disaster *saltus Teutoburgiensis* (*Annals* 1.60), which is often translated as Teutoburg Forest, but the Latin word *saltus* can mean 'woodland', 'pasture', 'glade', 'pass' or even 'ravine'. Curiously, the name also contains the root word *teuto*, evoking the spectre of the feared Teutones who invaded Italy at the end of the 2nd century BC. He locates *saltus Teutoburgiensis* 'not far' from a region 'between the Ems and the Lippe' (Tacitus, *Annals* 1.60) where the Bructeri nation lived.

It has been estimated that there are as many as 700 modern theories for the actual location of the battle. There are proponents for locations in the German state of Niedersachsen (Lower Saxony) in the vicinity of the Arnsberger Wald on the River Ruhr (*Rura*), the Beckumer Berge (Beckum Hills) on the River Lippe, the Teutoburger Wald and the Harz Mountains, as well as advocates for sites located in the state of Nordrhein-Westfalen (North Rhine-Westphalia) scattered over an arc of land from Unna, near Dortmund, to Bielefeld and Warstein – to as far west as the Netherlands.

The discovery of coins and military artefacts dating to the first decade of the 1st century AD in the Niewedder Senke (Niewedder Valley) near Osnabrück – originally proposed in the late 1800s by Theodor Mommsen and confirmed in the late 1990s by Tony Clunn – provides the most compelling support yet for the Kalkrieser Berg and the adjacent Große Moor as being a site in the four-day long battle conducted against Quinctilius Varus by Arminius.

A view of a forest near the Kalkrieser Berg in Lower Saxony, where some believe Arminius overwhelmed Varus in AD 9. Debate still continues over the exact location of the *Clades Variana*. Some 700 sites have been proposed. (Are Kolberg/CC BY-SA 3.0)

The legionary was most vulnerable on the march – a fact Arminius knew well. Normally the legionary marched in a column, in serried ranks and in step. He was expected to cover 20 miles in half a summer's day, but in wartime the rate was increased to 25 miles. Cassius Dio remarks that Varus' troops 'had with them many waggons and many beasts of burden as in time of peace; moreover, not a few women and children and a large retinue of servants were following them — one more reason for their advancing in scattered groups' (*Roman History* 56.20.1). The column of three legions, auxiliaries, baggage, attendants, slaves and camp followers was therefore long, stretching out over many miles. (Conrad Cichorius, 1896)

INTO COMBAT

At dawn the next day, the Roman army awoke to the familiar brassy sound of *cornicenes* sounding the reveille. Legionaries paired up to help each other to don their kit. One would bend forward to slip on his chain-mail suit, while the other pulled it down over his torso to ensure a snug fit; for men issued the new segmented plate armour, one held up the open kit as the wearer slipped inside and then manoeuvred to seat it comfortably on his shoulders, then attached the girdle plates by slipping the leather straps into the buckles at the front. Once kitted up, the men collapsed and rolled up their tents and guy ropes while others recovered the stakes from the parapet and tied them securely on the backs of the mules. Then the centurions bellowed out orders for the men to fall in behind their unit *signa*. Many men attached their helmets with a length of leather thong to a loop on the neckguard around their necks so that the headgear hung from the chest. It meant their heads were exposed, but carrying the helmet this way reduced neck strain. Each man picked up his large *scutum* – protected inside its leather cover – with his left hand and adjusted the carry strap, which would reduce the weight on his left hand on the march. Finally, each legionary picked up the two *pila* and a pole from which hung his personal effects and tools – a bronze saucepan (*trula*), basket, various tools, a length of chain, three days' rations and change of clothing. Thus weighed down with arms, armour and other gear the soldiers lived up to their nickname of 'Marius' Mules' after the consul who had made reforms in which the number of wheeled wagons was reduced to improve the speed of the Roman Army on the move but entailing the soldiers carrying more gear on their own backs.

Each century formed up into its cohorts and they, in turn, took their designated places behind the legionary eagles. When the horns sounded again the first legion in the line marched out into open country. It would take hours

for the last men of the army marching four or eight abreast to evacuate the field that had been its home the previous night.

Varus had still not received word from his Cheruscan auxiliaries, but he presumed they would arrive when they were able to. Unknown to Varus, Arminius had been executing the next phase of his plan. Surreptitiously the Germans had reached for their hidden weapons, turned on the Roman soldiers billeted at the road stations and staging posts in their communities and murdered them to a man. With the security forces neutralized the Germanic warriors then assembled for the journey to their designated place along the route of the governor's march – where they would wait, hidden among the trees and undergrowth, ready to strike at his unsuspecting troops.

The historian Cassius Dio criticizes Varus for poorly organizing his column and baggage train (*Roman History* 56.19.4). Though marching orders differed according to circumstances, a normal line-up in hostile territory was for the auxiliary cavalry and infantry to go well ahead of the main body. The vanguard comprised a single legion, chosen by lot. Behind them marched ten men from each century carrying the tools necessary for building a temporary camp. The pioneers, whose job it was to clear a track way for the advancing column, came next. Accompanied by a heavy escort the equipment of the general and his staff followed. The commander himself rode with his own personal bodyguard and staff of adjutants. The *ala* of cavalry from each legion rode as one body ahead of the mules that pulled the wagons carrying the artillery weapons. Following behind them, with an escort of picked troops, rode the legionary *legati* and military tribunes, and the *praefecti* of the auxiliary cohorts. Then came the remaining legions, led by their eagle standards and

Lightly equipped, highly manoeuvrable and quiet, the Cheruscan warrior could track the heavily equipped, slow-moving and noisy column of Roman troops without being noticed. His primary weapon was the *framea*, described by Tacitus as having 'an iron blade, short and narrow, but so sharp and manageable, that, as occasion requires, they employ it either in close or distant fighting' (*Germania* 6). The weapon could be thrust, stabbed or thrown and was used in combination with the shield. The iron tip could be leaf-shaped or barbed and made in various lengths. (Tony Austin/Project Germani)

then the musicians carrying their horns sloped over their shoulders. The legionaries marched six or more abreast as the terrain permitted. Protecting the rear of the column was a contingent of infantry, chosen by lot, and more mounted troops. Such a convoy would stretch over many miles. Normally non-combatants would follow the army, but Cassius Dio says traders, slaves, women, children and baggage train were all mixed up with Varus' troops and in no particular order.

Trusting that they were in friendly territory, the officers and men were unaware of the menace watching them from a distance. They marched on in relaxed mood. That afternoon, the Romans came under surprise attack. Showers of *framea* and stones seemed to come out of nowhere, striking the legionaries and non-Germanic auxiliaries. There were immediate casualties. The centurions maintained their cool and barked out orders to suppress the panic and maintain order. The legionaries' ability to respond was hindered by the bundle of personal effects each man carried over his left shoulder. They had to abandon them and quickly form up in defensive formations. As the adrenalin pumped into their veins, however, they seemed not to notice the added weight of the leather covers over their curved *scuta*. Meantime, those who had tied their bronze or iron helmets to their chests fumbled to detach them and quickly get their headgear on.

The Germanic warriors rushed to leverage the element of surprise and closed in on the Romans in their disorganized line. How many men Arminius' alliance was able to field is not known, but one reasoned estimate is 15,000 men. The greater number of warriors fought on foot, but they were joined by agile cavalry. The Germans brought to bear their many and varied weapons. Some launched slingshot; launched *en masse* at a packed body of men, stones could be devastating to unprotected flesh. The Germans' preferred weapon was the *framea*, a slender spear made in a variety of sizes, 3–9ft in length with a 4–8in iron blade at the tip. Some chose to throw their weapon over long distance. Others charged with the lance held overhead and thrust it forward at the target before them. Some charged with the *framea* locked under their right armpit like a jousting lance for maximum force on impact.

To Roman troops wearing standard-issue chain mail – still in widespread use at the time – this weapon would be particularly dangerous. Mail offered good protection from the long slashing sword favoured by the Gauls, but the sharp point of the Germans' favourite weapon could pierce and tear the shirts made of tiny riveted interlocking iron or bronze loops. The articulated, segmented plate armour (referred to as *lorica segmentata* by modern

The standard bearing the legionary eagle (*aquila*) was 'the chief ensign in the Roman armies and the standard of the whole legion' and 'always considered as sacred' (Vegetius, *On Military Matters* 2.6). It was the bird associated with Jupiter, the Romans' chief god, and an emblem of power and nobility. This silver coin – minted for *Legio* II when it served under *triumvir* Marcus Antonius – shows the eagle, with its wings stretched upwards, between two cohort standards (*signa*). At Teutoburg the Germans captured the eagles of all three of Varus' legions, causing the Romans great shame (*infamia*). (Roma Numismatics)

historians, but almost certainly not called that by the Romans) may have been invented to provide the greater protection needed from Germanic weaponry and styles of combat. Indeed, the earliest known remnants of this plate armour were found at Dangstetten and dated to 9 BC – contemporary with Drusus the Elder's campaigns in the Alps and Bavarian hills – while other fragments have been found at the Kalkrieser Berg, near Osnabrück, and dated to c. AD 9.

The only Roman historian to mention the weather at the time of the battle of Teutoburg Pass is Cassius Dio, who wrote some 200 years after the massacre: 'meanwhile a violent rain and wind came up that separated them still further, while the ground, that had become slippery around the roots and logs, made walking very treacherous for them, and the tops of the trees kept breaking off and falling down, causing much confusion' (*Roman History* 56.20.3). Velleius Paterculus – who lived at the time of the events and gives the earliest account of them – does not even mention the weather, and neither does the near-contemporary historian Florus. Dio was likely drawing on a Roman stereotype that Germania was cold and wet. Tacitus observes in his book on Germania, 'their country, though somewhat various in appearance, yet generally either bristles with forests or reeks with swamps; it is more rainy on the side of Gallia, bleaker on that of Noricum and Pannonia' (*Germania* 5). Tacitus is the only Roman historian to call the location by the name *saltus Teutoburgiensis* (*Annals* 1.60) – where *saltus* can mean pass and ravine as well as glade, pasture or woodland – but does so in the context of the visit to the site several years later by Germanicus Caesar. These ancient-world stereotypes and ambiguities of language obscure the details of the battles.

Other Germanic warriors now in close-quarters combat swung their spears in a wide arc, back and forth, forcing their opponents to step back to avoid the deadly blows. A menacing swooshing sound accompanied the manoeuvre as the iron-tipped point atop the wooden shaft sliced through the air. Other German warriors wielded single-edged swords or machetes with which they slashed and chopped at their opponents' unprotected arms and legs. A well-aimed slicing cut to the forearm could force a man to drop his *gladius*, or a stab to the thigh or calf could bring a man to his knees.

The Germans had planned their attack well. They sealed off Varus' escape route – the way the Romans had come – leaving Varus only one way out: forward and deeper into their trap. However, his advance was hampered by the supply-line of animals, wagons and non-combatants, now panicking under the attack, mixed in among his regular troops. The legionaries instinctively attempted to defend themselves and stand their ground. They divided down their line and turned to face the enemy. Those that could unleashed their *pila* and formed up with their *gladii* drawn and shields held high. But then, according to Cassius Dio, a strong wind blew up and it began to rain heavily (*Roman History* 56.20.3). It was not long before the Roman troops and their shield covers were sodden. They struggled to hold the heavy *scuta* steady as the wind tugged at them like kites. Though the Roman legionaries were tired, their discipline held and the men battled on.

Varus knew he needed to get his men to a defensible space and ordered that a camp be pitched. A suitable clearing was located on a rise among the trees. While some troops fought, their comrades dug, both under a constant hail of slingshot and spears. Almost as suddenly as they had appeared, the Germans vanished into the forest. The Romans retreated behind the protective cover of their hastily dug entrenchments. The senior officers gathered for a meeting with their commander. Arminius was still absent, presumed missing in action. Varus ordered that the baggage train be abandoned – a command typically only ordered in a time of crisis – so that the men could move faster. The priority was to get to Fort Aliso. Shocked by the turn of events, the men ate their rations, planned their next move and tried to sleep.

OPPOSITE
Perhaps the most poignant memorial of the Battle of Teutoburg Pass to survive is the gravestone of centurion Marcus Caelius. The inscription (*CIL* 13.8648) reads 'M[arcus] Caelius, son of Titus, of the Lemonian voting tribe, from Bononia [Bologna], first centurion of *Legio* XIIX. [He was] 53½ years old. He fell in the Varian War. His bones may be interred here. P[ublius] Caelius, son of Titus, of the Lemonian voting tribe, his brother, erected [this monument]'. Caelius is shown with several military decorations: a *corona civilis*, which he received because he saved a citizen's life, a gold *torque* on each shoulder, *armillae* on his wrists and five *phalerae* on his chest. The stele was found at Birten in 1620 and confirms that *Legio* XIIX was stationed at Vetera, a fortress founded by Drusus the Elder on the hill now known as Fürstenberg, Xanten. (Agnete)

Arminius

Arminius, also known as Hermann (18/17 BC–AD 21), was son of chief Segimerus of the Cherusci (Velleius Paterculus, *Roman History* 2.118.1). He may have been taken as a hostage under a peace treaty negotiated with Tiberius Caesar in 7 BC whereafter he was raised and educated in Rome as a citizen. Intelligent and charismatic, when old enough he was given command of his own ethnic unit of cavalry and probably saw service with the Roman Army during the Great Illyrian Revolt (AD 6–9). For personal reasons during that period he switched loyalties and conceived a plan to ally his own nation with neighbouring Germanic tribes in an uprising, using his first-hand knowledge of Roman strategies and tactics against them.

By AD 9 Arminius was 26 or 27 years old. He likely led a unit of his own countrymen in action during the Illyrian (AKA Batonian) War in the western Balkans. It is unclear what made him eventually decide to betray his Roman masters though the ancient historians believed it was the imposition of tribute upon the Germans. He secretly assembled an alliance of German nations with his native Cherusci tribe under his own leadership. The ensuing ambush at Teutoburg Pass is one of the most studied battles in military history. This imaginative portrait of Arminius is part of the architecture of the Kaiserbahnhof, Bad Homburg in Hesse, which opened in 1860. (Reinhard Dietrich/CC BY-SA 3.0)

As dawn broke on the morning of the third day of the German revolt, the Romans evacuated their camp. Varus' aim now was to get some distance between his and the enemy's forces and reach the fortified positions on the Lippe and the Rhine as fast as possible. The plan appeared to work. The Roman army emerged out of the forest into open country. Fortune was believed to favour the bold. The nimbler units advanced quickly, leaving the slower ones and the non-combatant stragglers further behind. The Roman line was now thinning out – all the easier for Arminius' allies to break it into smaller groups and cut them down. The Germans attacked again and kept up their assault through the rest of the day. Terrain, time and even the weather were all on Arminius' side. The Romans reached the end of the open plain and before them was dense forest. They had no choice but to enter it. Between its trees the next group of Germanic warriors was waiting to attack them. The legionaries and auxiliary infantry tried to form up but in the confined space the cavalry got in their way. Unable to muster a stout defence, the Romans suffered yet more casualties. Now without supplies and entrenching tools, the men did the best they could to form a defensible space in which to take refuge. Under the night sky Varus and his officers assessed their desperate situation. Lucius Eggius, one of the legionary officers, proposed surrender, but he was overruled. Romans did not surrender to barbarian bandits.

After a difficult and restless night, the fourth day began with more rainfall. Soaked to the bone, the troops faced the uncertainty of the day ahead.

Publius Quinctilius Varus

Publius Quinctilius Varus (46 BC–AD 9) came from an impoverished noble family in Cremona yet ascended the Roman politico-military career ladder with some distinction. He served as *legatus* of *Legio* XIX in the Alpine War of 15 BC under Tiberius and Nero Claudius Drusus. Consul in 13 BC jointly with Tiberius, he competently administered the province of Africa (8–7 BC) and as governor of Syria (7–4 BC) he proved a decisive military commander by putting down a major revolt in Iudaea – skills recognized when Caesar Augustus appointed him in AD 6 to continue the pacification of the new province of Germania. There he dutifully executed his mission of implementing Roman policy.

The ligatured letters V A R stamped on this low-denomination bronze coin over the profile of Emperor Augustus spell the name Varus. Quinctilius Varus was Augustus' representative in Germania responsible for nation building, ensuring internal security and promoting Roman interests. Authorized to wield delegated military power (*imperium*) he was commander of five legions – including XIIX and XIX – and an unknown number of auxiliary units. (Goethe-Universität Frankfurt, Institut für Archäologische Wissenschaften)

It was not long before the Germans moved in. Relentlessly they inflicted casualties on the Romans, who staggered on with grim determination. Relying on their discipline and training, they would not give up. In the struggle Eggius fell. Perhaps it was on this day too that 53-year old centurion Marcus Caelius of *Legio* XIIX died (*CIL* 13.8648). As centurions fell, their hand-picked *optiones* assumed command. With casualties mounting it was becoming grimly evident that every man must now fend for himself. Paterculus records the attempt of Numonius Vala, *legatus* of one of the three legions, to break out with his scouts. He did not get far before he and his men were cut down (Velleius Paterculus, *Roman History* 2.119.4). There were astonishing acts of heroism. Paterculus tells of one legionary, named Caldus Caelius, who, having been taken captive by the Germans and realizing the terrible fate that awaited him, struck his own head using the iron prisoner's chain around his neck, and killed himself (Velleius Paterculus, *Roman History* 2.120.6). Legionary *signifer* Arrius grabbed the *aquila* from off its pole to avert the disgrace of it falling into the enemy's hands (Crinagoras, *Palatine Anthology* 7.741). He tucked the eagle in his clothing and managed to hide in a blood-soaked marsh (Florus, *Epitome* 2.30.38). (Despite his gallantry the eagle was nevertheless later captured by the Germans.) Believing he might be shown mercy by his captors, one officer, Ceionius, surrendered (Velleius Paterculus, *Roman History* 2.119.4). What happened to him is not recorded, but the fate facing any Romans who were taken alive was gruesome. Blood offerings and human sacrifice were widely practised among the Germanic people. Prisoners could expect their eyes to be gouged out and their heads nailed to tree trunks while they were

The battle of Teutoburg Pass stunned an ancient nation and inspired a modern one. Starting with Martin Luther in the 16th century, the *Hermannschlacht* (German for 'Arminius' Battle') was used by proponents working for a united Germany in the 18th and 19th centuries and was the subject of many popular stage plays and works of art. The original of this painting, called *Der Triumph Hermanns nach seinem Sieg über Varus*, was completed by famous German painter Johann Heinrich Tischbein in the 1750s. (Public domain)

still alive. Florus preserves the tragic tale – perhaps apocryphal – of one legionary who, having had his tongue cut out, saw it waved in front of him by the German responsible. 'At last, you viper,' the German is alleged to have said, 'you have ceased to hiss' (Florus, *Epitome* 2.30.37). The man's lips were then sewn together.

Rather than be taken prisoner, Varus and his officers decided to commit suicide. To prevent its desecration Varus' adjutants attempted to burn their commander's lifeless body, but they were only partially successful. The Germans found the charred remains, cut off the head and presented it to Arminius. He sent it to Marboduus of the Marcomanni, hoping he would join the cause and declare war on Rome. In the event he did not and sent the head to Augustus. The war spoils were divided among the rebel alliance. To the Bructeri went the prized *aquila* of *Legio* XIX. The Chauci and Marsi were also each given one. The German warriors stripped the Roman dead of their valuable body armour and weapons and used them to equip themselves.

Remarkably, there were Roman survivors. Some were enslaved by their Germanic captors, but others reached Fort Aliso and then made for the Rhine, where they told their tales of horror amid the German forests.

Idistaviso

Summer AD 16

BACKGROUND TO BATTLE

Arriving from the western Balkans in late AD 9, in the immediate aftermath of the 'Varian Disaster' Tiberius appointed his adopted son Germanicus Caesar to take command of what was left of the Rhine army – still under Asprenas – until he could return with reinforcements. In the event the feared invasion of Germanic tribes did not occur and the Rhine again became the northernmost frontier of the empire. Tiberius and Germanicus undertook punitive raids across the river, but no serious attempt was made to retake lost Roman territories. In AD 13 Germanicus was appointed *legatus Augusti pro praetore* of the three Gallic provinces and the army of the Rhine now divided between two new military districts, Germania Inferior and Germania Superior. The mission Augustus assigned him, according to Velleius Paterculus, was 'to put an end to such traces of the war as still remained' (*Roman History* 2.123.1). When the legions learned of the death of Augustus in August AD 14 and of the succession of Tiberius, the legions of Germania Inferior mutinied. Germanicus moved quickly to deal with the matter. At issue were pay and conditions. Germanicus resolved the 'industrial dispute' and to re-establish discipline and unit cohesion he led the army in a punitive raid against the Marsi on the right bank of the Rhine.

Encouraged by the success of the mission, he conceived a plan to avenge Teutoburg. The following year he launched an offensive against the Chatti, allies of the Cherusci, and defeated them, razing their capital and devastating their land. In late spring he received a message from Segestes – the man who had informed Varus of Arminius' plot – who now feared for his life. Germanicus launched a snatch raid and rescued the ally. He also captured

After the German Revolt of AD 9 the north-western frontier changed beyond recognition. The Roman army had evacuated the lands east of the Rhine, abandoning all its camps along the Lahn (*Laugona*), Lippe and Main rivers, and retreated back to the winter camps originally founded by Nero Claudius Drusus Germanicus. Two new military districts had been carved out of Gallia Belgica. The army units in Germania Superior (Upper Germany), administered from Mogontiacum (modern Mainz) under Caius Silius, guarded the Rhine from its source in the Alps to the mid-section. The army of Germania Inferior (Lower Germany), administered from Ara Ubiorum (Cologne) under Aulus Caecina Severus, protected the river from the middle section to its outflow in the North Sea. Both men reported to Germanicus Caesar as the *legatus Augusti pro praetore* and had four legions apiece. A fleet of ships (*classis Germanica*) patrolled the river.

Still loyal to Rome were the Angrivarii, Batavi, Cananefates, Chauci, Cugerni, Frisii and Marcomanni. Standing with the Cherusci were the Chatti. The Marsi had been subjected to a brutal punitive raid by Germanicus to restore unit cohesion after he quelled a mutiny of the legions of Germania Inferior in AD 14. The Marcomanni continued to uphold their treaty with Rome.

On the eve of the new campaign Germanicus Caesar faced having to take men and matériel into hostile Germania Libera to wage war against the allies of Arminius of the Cherusci. As they had done for his father, the rivers of Germany offered Germanicus routes to deliver military resources using river craft. He conceived a multi-pronged attack from the Rhine along the Ems and Lippe rivers to surround the Cherusci, and overland to cut them off from the Chatti. The Angrivarii would yet prove disloyal.

Thusnelda, wife of Arminius. War with the Germanic hero was inevitable. Germanicus divided his forces into three groups, one taking a route by sea, the others going overland, to surround the Germanic tribe. *En route* the *aquila* of *Legio* XIX was found among the Bructeri. The groups converged on the site of the final battle at Teutoburg Pass. The bones of the fallen were gathered up and ceremoniously buried and a mound of earth thrown over them. On the return trips there were skirmishes with the Cherusci. At Pontes Longi (Long Bridges) – an abandoned 'corduroy' or plank road constructed by Domitius Ahenobarbus – the army group under Aulus Caecina Severus found itself trapped before managing to break away free, but lost all its equipment in the escape. Along the Frisian coast Germanicus' troops and supplies were scattered when the tide came in. Only Lucius Stertinius made it back to the Rhine without incident. Over the winter Germanicus constructed a new fleet of 1,000 ships, including barges and transports, re-equipped his troops, replaced the lost horses and planned a new campaign.

In AD 16 Germanicus' army of *c.* 52,000 men prepared to invade Germania again, this time intent on taking Arminius alive or dead. When he received

Having quelled a mutiny of the Rhine Army, Germanicus personally led his men across the Rhine in campaigns against Arminius. This picture, from Trajan's Column, shows a Roman commander on a tribunal speaking to his troops (*ad locutio*). In part the German War (AD 15–16) was a means of restoring discipline, morale and unit cohesion among the legions, but it was also a serious attempt to reclaim the lost territory by breaking the German alliance. Addressing the men before action was common practice at this time, though Augustus discouraged his sons from referring to them as 'fellow soldiers' (*comilitiones*). (Conrad Cichorius, 1896)

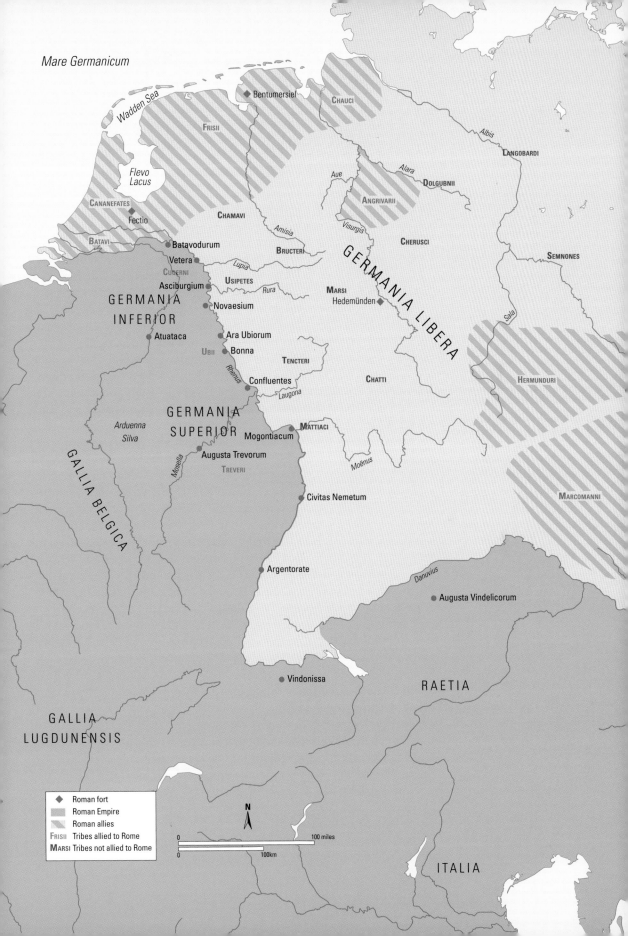

Mare Germanicum

Wadden Sea

Flevo
Lacus

BENTUMERSIEL

FRISII

CHAUCI

Albis

LANGOBARDI

Aue

Alara

DOLGUBNII

ANGRIVARII

Amisia

Visurgis

CHERUSCI

SEMNONES

CANANEFATES

Fectio

CHAMAVI

BATAVI

Batavodurum

Vetera

CUBERNI

GERMANIA
INFERIOR

Lupia

BRUCTERI

GERMANIA LIBERA

Asciburgium

USIPETES

Rura

MARSI
Hedemünden

Novaesium

Atuataca

Ara Ubiorum

Sala

UBII

Bonna

TENCTERI

Rhenus

Confluentes

CHATTI

HERMUNDURI

Laugona

GERMANIA
SUPERIOR

Arduenna
Silva

Mogontiacum

MATTIACI

Augusta Trevorum

TREVERI

Mosella

Moënus

GALLIA BELGICA

Civitas Nemetum

MARCOMANNI

Argentorate

Danuvius

Augusta Vindelicorum

GALLIA
LUGDUNENSIS

Vindonissa

RAETIA

N

◆ Roman fort
▨ Roman Empire
▨ Roman allies
FRISII Tribes allied to Rome
MARSI Tribes not allied to Rome

0   100 miles
0   100km

ITALIA

word that a fort on the Lippe was being besieged, Germanicus himself led six legions and cohorts of auxiliaries across the Rhine to relieve it. Entrenchments were then constructed between Fort Aliso and the Rhine. Meanwhile scouts were sent out to locate Arminius. They found him in a field on the River Weser (*Visurgis*). Germanicus brought his army up on the opposite bank, ready to take on his adversary.

Germanicus Caesar found his enemy standing on the opposite bank of the Weser with his war council. There followed a bizarre incident. Arminius approached and asked the Roman commander whether he could speak with his brother, Flavus. Germanicus agreed and also pulled his foot-archers out of range so they could not strike down the German war chief. Flavus was the kind of 'barbarian' the Romans nurtured. He was *dux* of a cohort of his own countrymen and had successfully assimilated the Roman way of life and spoke Latin with some fluency. For his loyalty he had been rewarded with increased pay, military awards for valour in battle – including a neck chain and a crown – and other undisclosed gifts. His rebel brother belittled Flavus' achievements as poor payoffs for giving up his freedom and heritage. The Roman commander, and the armies of both sides, watched the increasingly bitter squabble from a distance. Spoiling for a fight, Flavus demanded his weapons and horse, but was finally interrupted by a senior officer, Lucius Stertinius, who tapped Flavus on the shoulder and ended the public altercation. The brothers parted and with them their armies, which returned to their camps for the night.

Next morning the forces of Free Germania and Rome took up their positions. The Germanic army assembled opposite the Romans on the right bank, on a plain sloping down to the river, with forest behind them. Roman *exploratores* had been dispatched to find out the size of the enemy and its location. Germanicus assessed his options. To engage the enemy the Roman commander's army would have to cross the river. Tacitus reports that the river was shallow and that there were fords in places; Germanicus decided, however, that without bridges to cross it he would be exposing his legionaries in their heavy armour to unnecessary risk. This day the legionaries would stand and watch. His best option was to use mounted troops. He ordered his *primus pilus*, Aemilius, and *praefectus*, Stertinius, each to launch flanking attacks with their respective cavalry units. They would provide decoys for a direct frontal attack by his finest cavalry directed at Arminius' centre. The honour of executing that main thrust would go to the cohorts of Batavi under their leader Chariovalda.

The Batavi – an offshoot of the Chatti – were renowned for their expert riding skills and courage. When Aemilius, Stertinius and their men crossed the river the Germans responded. Now distracted, Chariovalda charged into the river 'where the stream is most rapid' (Tacitus, *Annals* 2.11) at the head of his own men and made straight for the Cherusci. Arminius was not so easily duped. Having himself served with the Romans he was fully familiar with this multipronged attack strategy. Anticipating the Romans' move, he had set a trap of his own. He had succeeded in luring Chariovalda's men onto the plain. Then he sprung his trap.

From the cover of the forest out rushed the Cheruscan infantry. When they were in range, they launched their *frameae*. The deadly lances hurtled through the air and rained down on the unsuspecting Batavi cavalry, which took casualties. Rushing towards the oncoming auxiliary cavalry, other warriors on foot charged forward and thrust their spears at the horses and their mounts, inflicting deep wounds when they struck flesh. Chariovalda shouted his order to rally his troops into a tight formation above the cries and screams of men and the clash of metal and wood. The Germans now launched another lethal barrage of missiles. In the midst of the mêlée, both the Batavian chief and his horse were struck and killed. Many of his Batavian war band fell amid the same iron rain of death. Witnessing the massacre of their comrades, Stertinius and Aemilius wheeled round their mounted contingents. Their quick action saved the Batavi from complete annihilation, and the German auxiliary cavalry was able to disengage from the Germanic assault.

While the action unfolded Germanicus had crossed the river in person and taken a position on the right bank. From there he surveyed the unfolding battle. It did not look good. He quickly realized that his stratagem had failed. He could have thrown more men into the fight, but wisely decided against committing additional forces that day. He ordered a retreat and, crossing the river again, returned in disappointment to the camp. The battle was over.

Germanicus now came unexpectedly into useful intelligence. A deserter from the German side presented himself in the Roman camp. Under questioning, the man revealed that Arminius had decided the place and time for the next battle and that other alliance tribes were gathering in a forest grove sacred to Hercules. Germanicus' own scouts returned and confirmed the truth of the deserter's statements. From the informant, the commander also learned that the Germans' plan was to attack the Romans at night while they slept in their tents. Armed with this critical information Germanicus considered his options: to hold his ground or to retreat.

Battles can be won or lost on the morale of the soldiers. The Roman commander determined that he needed first to assess the mood of his men before deciding which course of action to take. He disguised himself as an animal handler and wandered around the camp to listen to his soldiers

Germanicus Iulius Caesar

The son of Nero Claudius Drusus Germanicus, the general who attempted the first serious and systematic conquest of Germania Magna, Germanicus (16 BC–AD 19) began his military career relatively late, at age 22, when he successfully led troops in the Great Illyrian Revolt (Batonian War) of AD 6–9. In AD 14 he put down a mutiny of the legions in Germania Inferior. To restore unit cohesion he led a punitive raid against the Marsi and over the following two years led campaigns against Arminius and his Germanic allies to avenge the massacre at Teutoburg Pass. Willing to lead his men from the front, he was popular with his troops yet unwaveringly loyal to his commander-in-chief.

At the start of his German War in AD 15, Germanicus Caesar, aged 31, was a charismatic public figure, a talented orator and an accomplished writer. He was married to Augustus' second granddaughter Vispania Agrippina (Agrippina the Elder), a strong-willed woman who accompanied him on his provincial assignments. She bore nine children. One was Caius (born AD 12) who was beloved of the men of the Rhine legions, who nicknamed him 'Caligula' – 'little boot' – after his child-size military-style footwear. (© Karwansaray)

as they spoke from the heart. The legionaries spoke openly of Germanicus' nobility, endurance and even-handed manner. They expressed their loyalty to him and swore to punish the men who had broken the peace for which the Roman forces had fought so hard. Proof of their sincerity was to come in an unexpected form. In the middle of the night, a Germanic warrior rode up to the Roman entrenchments and shouted to the men inside in Latin. To each Roman who switched to the German side he promised a wife, land and pay of 100 *sestertii* for every day the war lasted. From the parapet the Roman troops jeered the man. They shouted back that they would take the land of the Germans and with it *their* wives as spoils of war.

Their fighting talk was heartening for Germanicus to hear. Tacitus records that bolstering his confidence was a favourable dream the Roman commander had that same night. Frequently used by ancient historians simply as a literary device, dreams were nevertheless taken seriously by many Romans, who considered the interpretation of them as prophetic. What *is* true is that when he awoke next morning Germanicus had made up his mind. The army of Rome would stay and fight the Germans.

The duties of a Roman commander included observing religious rituals. Germanicus was an *augur*, trained to interpret the flight of birds. Covering his head respectfully with a fold of his cloak and clasping the ritual crooked

Flavus

Flavus was likely handed over as a hostage by his father Segimerus at the same time as his older brother Arminius. His Latin name, which means 'yellow' or 'golden', probably refers to the colour of his hair, suggesting that he cut a striking figure. He is described as 'a man famous for his loyalty, and for having lost an eye by a wound, a few years ago, when Tiberius was in command' (Tacitus, *Annals* 2.9). Like Arminius he was a *dux* or commander of a (mixed?) unit of ethnic cavalry or infantry. The facial wound was sustained in a campaign when he fought with the Romans. He received 'increased pay, a neck chain, a crown, and other military gifts' (Tacitus, *Annals* 2.9), which were much sought-after awards given to Roman troops for courage and gallantry shown on the battlefield. After the public contretemps with his brother across the Weser he disappears from history.

The Roman Army drew on the skills and talents of its subject nations and treaty allies. Flavus was a decorated and respected commander, probably of a unit of cavalry (like this rider on Trajan's Column) or a mixed cohort of horse and foot soldiers. He was a fiercely loyal servant of the Roman Empire and was prepared to confront his brother, Arminius, in public at the Weser River over the latter's desertion to the German side. (Conrad Cichorius, 1896)

staff in his hand, Germanicus raised his arms, gazed up at the sky and took the auspices. He determined them to be favourable and then called for the soldiers to fall in. From a tribunal he addressed them, using his skills as an orator to rouse his men to wreak havoc upon the poorly armed Germanic host. It is unlikely that many of the regular troops heard his words, but the men cheered their leader enthusiastically nevertheless. He gave the order for the horns to sound and the centurions barked orders to stand to attention. Behind their ditch, earthen rampart and parapet of sharpened wooden stakes, the Roman troops had formed up tightly in their centuries and cohorts. In their serried lines the legionaries waited beside their unit insignia for their enemy to arrive. Hours passed. Finally, at midday a party of Germanic infantry and cavalry arrived. If the appearance of the enemy army was intended to strike fear into the Romans it failed. When they withdrew Germanicus gave the order for the army to march out of the camp and prepare for battle. Roman infantry and cavalry waded across the river. Legionaries needed to take care. Their iron hobnailed boots could slip on the wet stones or, with each man carrying his heavy *scutum* in his left hand, without deft footwork they could lose their balance on an uneven surface. Having successfully negotiated the river they scrambled up the bank onto the grassy plain above.

1 0900hrs (approx.): Arminius assembles his troops on the high ground, with his Cherusci retainers at the centre and his Angrivarian allies on the flanks.

2 0900hrs (approx.): Germanicus Caesar arrays his troops by legion and cohort on the sloping plain. Foot archers form up in front. Behind them stand Gallic, Raetic and Vindelician auxiliaries. Forming the next line are four legions and Caesar himself with his two Praetorian Cohorts and cavalry on the wings. The remaining four legions, auxiliary cohorts and *alae* make up the rear line.

3 1000hrs (approx.): Arminius gives the order for his men to charge down the hillside using their momentum to smash through the Roman lines.

4 1005hrs (approx.): The Roman archers loose a rolling enfilade at the approaching Germans, who take casualties but continue at speed towards the bowmen.

5 1015hrs (approx.): The Roman cavalry under command of Aemilius and Stertinius ride up the slope to attempt to encircle the Germans.

6 1030hrs (approx.): Fearing the foot-archers may be overrun, the Gallic, Raetic and Vindelician auxiliaries advance to come to the aid of their vulnerable comrades. The Cherusci and their allies engage the Roman troops.

7 1100hrs (approx.): Germanicus gives the order for a general advance of the remaining Roman units. Mêlée ensues as the two sides battle each other.

8 1200hrs (approx.): Arminius breaks through the Roman vanguard. Though he is recognized by some Chauci auxiliaries in the service of Rome, they let him pass unhindered. Germanic and Roman forces struggle to gain the upper hand in fierce close-quarters combat through the afternoon.

9 1800hrs (approx.): Sensing the battle is lost, the Germanic troops begin to flee the battle space. The Romans pursue them up the hill and into the forest. Some attempt to cross the Weser to safety, while others climb trees hoping to hide, but are shot down by Roman archers. Arminius and Inguiomerus escape. At 1930hrs (approx.), Germanicus Caesar claims victory for Tiberius and the troops acclaim him *imperator*.

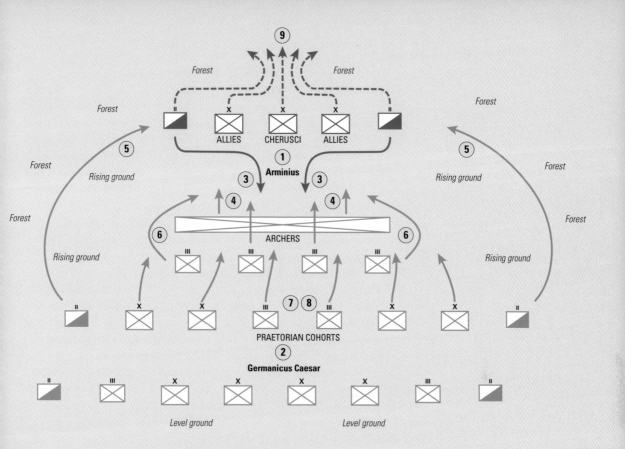

Battlefield environment

The Roman historian Tacitus describes the site of the battle as 'a plain [campus]' which 'winds between the Weser and a hill range, its breadth varying as the river banks recede or the spurs of the hills project on it' (Annals 2.16). He adds 'in their rear rose a forest, with the branches rising to a great height, while there were clear spaces between the trunks. The barbarian army occupied the plain and the outskirts of the wood' (Annals 2.16).

Tacitus specifically calls the place by its ancient name Idistaviso. Etymological analysis by modern scholars suggests the word means 'the forest meadow goddesses'. However, the 'dista' in the name may refer to the Deister, a chain of hills in Lower Saxony running from the town of Springe in the south to Rodenberg in the north and rising to a height of 1,300ft. There are several theories for the location of the actual site of the battle. Sites north of the town of Minden such as Döhren or Petershagen have been proposed, while other proponents favour locations on the eastern bank of the River Weser, such as at Oldendorf or Rinteln or Wiedensahl.

The exact location of Idistaviso, like so many other ancient battle sites, still eludes historians. One theory is that the name is a Latinization of the old German *Deister-Wiese*, 'Meadow of the Deister'. The Deister is a chain of hills in Lower Saxony, 30 miles east of Minden. The chain has a total length of 14 miles and today is still well wooded. It is viewed here from the west at Lauenau. (Tortuosa/CC BY-SA 3.0)

INTO COMBAT

On dry land the legions and cohorts deployed according to the plan upon which Germanicus and his officers had agreed. Tacitus is our only source for the battle. He does not detail the exact positions of the legions and Praetorians, but from his outline the general plan can be deduced. The army arrayed itself in three ranks (*triplex acies*). The cohorts of Gallic and Germanic auxiliaries were placed in the van with the foot-archers (*sagittarii*). In the second rank behind them stood four legions and Germanicus Caesar himself with his two *Cohortes Praetoriae* and some picked cavalry. In the third rank were the other four legions, the lightly armed troops with horse-archers and the remaining cohorts of men recruited from the allies. Then they stood and waited.

The battle at Idistaviso was initiated by Arminius. Looking down at their enemy laid out in a chequerboard formation on the ground below, the warriors of the Cherusci and their alliance partners stood side by side. To frighten their foes and embolden their own spirits the men screamed out the *barritus* and struck their *frameae* and swords rhythmically against their wooden shields decorated with colourful blazons. In their cloaks, tunics and trousers they presented a lively front. The menacing noise echoed across the plain. Arminius chose the time. The Germanic horns blasted their shrill tones and the infantry of the Angrivarii and Cherusci charged *en masse* at the Roman line. Separating the two sides was several hundred feet of open green space. Seeing the Germans make their move, Germanicus ordered his cavalry under Stertinius to attack the Germans on their flanks and rear. The momentum of the German charge gathered pace and the space between the opponents quickly narrowed. Inserting the cavalry among the German infantry, both inflicted casualties and slowed down their charge. Galloping up the incline, Stertinius' unit veered to engage the Germanic infantry on their unprotected side. Roman cavalry did not have stirrups but the design of their square saddle, with raised horns of bronze covered with leather in each

A massed German charge with the *framea* was a formidable form of attack. At Idistaviso 'the Cherusci were posted by themselves on the high ground, so as to rush down on the Romans during the battle' (Tacitus, *Annals* 2.17). To intercept them before they crashed into the legionary ranks, Germanicus sent in Stertinius with other cavalry *turmae* to make a detour and attack them on their unprotected rear. (Tony Austin/Project Germani)

corner, provided the stability the riders needed to use their weapons with lethal effect. They charged among the running warriors, impaling many with their lances (*hasta, lancea*). Once these were discharged, the cavalrymen unsheathed their 23–33in-long *spathae*, which they used to slash down on the enemy foot-soldiers, most of whom did not wear helmets.

For the time being Germanicus held his infantry back. His legionaries stood, watching the battle unfold, but keenly awaiting the command to advance. Germanicus scanned the battle space. Momentarily he spotted eight eagles in the sky. The eagle held great significance for the Romans. It was the bird of Jupiter and the iconic emblem carried by each of the legions. As a trained *augur*, Germanicus knew how to play this unexpected appearance to his advantage. It was time to let the infantry auxiliaries and legionaries play their part. 'Go!' he shouted to his men as the birds flew towards the woods and swept into them, 'Follow the Roman birds, the true deities of our legions!' (Tacitus, *Annals* 2.17). The brassy blasts of Roman horns sounding the order to advance filled the air. The soldiers of the first and second ranks stood to attention. At the same instant the centurions called out the order, the *signa* flashed as sunlight caught the polished metal work as they were jerked up and tilted forwards by their standard bearers. Without hesitation the men moved forward in unison.

Well ahead of the legionaries the foot-archers had come within firing range and halted. With their practised skill, each took an arrow from the quiver that hung at his side, slipped the notch at the end of the slender missile into the bowstring and pulled it back. Their unit commander gave the order to release. As the archers let go the string the energy stored in the bow, a composite laminate of wood and horn glued together, propelled the arrows. The iron-tipped missiles sliced through the air at the oncoming body of massed German infantry. Some projectiles missed their targets or pierced shields, but others struck the warriors full-on with deadly force.

The legionaries advancing behind them maintained a steady speed. Their centurions called out the pace. The sound of metal, leather and wood clapping against each other mingled with the cries and shouts of the men already in the thick of battle ahead. When they reached the kill zone they halted. On the centurions' command, each legionary brought his *scutum* across the front of his body, switched one of his two *pila* from his right hand to his left and then returned to his upright position. On the centurion's mark, each legionary turned slightly, leaned back, and using the shield as a counterweight, unleashed his first *pilum*. The air filled with shafts of iron and wood, landing in the ranks of charging Germans. With each man now switching his second *pilum* into his right hand, the legionaries repeated the move with the same deadly effect. The Germans immediately took casualties. The pyramid-shaped head of the *pilum* smashed through the fibres of the wooden planks of the warriors' shields and kinetic energy drove the slender iron deeper into their shields. The enemy soldier could try to remove the *pilum* or abandon his shield, but either way the momentum of the German charge had now been broken. The unlucky ones were wounded or killed by the Roman missile attack.

Centurions of the front-line Roman units bellowed out the order to form up in wedges. These would punch through the German line and engage the

'Follow the Roman birds!'

Roman view: Up until this moment Idistaviso had been a largely auxiliary battle. After *Cohortes Gallorum*, *Raetorum* and *Vindelicorum* had succeeded in chasing off the German warriors who had encircled the Roman foot-archers, the legionaries were sent in to finish the job. Earlier that day the Roman commander, Germanicus Caesar, had exhorted his men to follow eight eagles that he had spotted in the sky, an augury of good fortune for his side.

Seeing the Germans re-assembled in a shield wall, the tribune in the middle distance has ordered his centurions in the first rank to form their units up in a series of *cunei* – wedges – fanning out from the centurion. Like an arrowhead the individual wedge formation concentrates the strike force at a single point, and tears through the target. The men clutch their bayonet-like double-edged swords to the side and hold their curved shields up to eye-level. Initially striding in unison up the incline of the battlefield, when just a few yards from the Germans the centurion gave the order to run. Now, as the *cornu* blasts, the men let out a shrill war cry while racing forward. Using the momentum of the charge to disrupt the integrity of the enemy line, they will then engage in hand-to-hand combat.

Germanic view: The Germans' direct attack – led by Arminius, even though wounded himself – has almost succeeded in wiping out the Roman foot-archers, but has been foiled by the unexpected arrival of mixed cavalry and infantry. Throwing the scene into confusion, 'two columns of the [German] enemy fled in opposite directions, that, which had occupied the wood, rushing into the open, those who had been drawn up on the plains, into the wood. The Cherusci, who were between them, were dislodged from the hills' (Tacitus, *Annals* 2.18).

Despite this setback the Germans are still spoiling for a fight. The Cherusci warriors have formed up in a dense mass around their battle standard. Their use of shields and long spears presents the oncoming enemy with an impenetrable shield wall. If they can just hold the formation they might yet be able to repel the Romans and take back the field. Some warriors join in the *barritus*, an intimidating war song evoking past glories and raising their own spirits. Others strike the inside of their shields rhythmically in time with the beat of the song. This is what they live for – a chance to display their courage before their war chief, to win bragging rights after the battle and receive a share of the spoils.

enemy in hand-to-hand combat, where the Romans' short stabbing swords would do most damage. Each unit of legionaries re-aligned on either side of their centurion, dressing their line so that they formed two angled sides of an arrowhead. With their shields up high they unsheathed their *gladii* and held them ready to thrust as required by Roman combat doctrine.

As the Roman infantry advanced, Stertinius' cavalry was still nipping at the rear of the Germanic lines. The assault led by the Cherusci was now in disarray. Their massed charge had failed. Panic began to grip the men who had charged the Roman centre so confidently just minutes before. Many turned and ran back towards the protection of the forest above the plain. However, others, up until then hidden among trees and waiting for their chance for glory, now rushed out towards the Romans. Chaos ensued as men running from the field collided with others running onto it. Arminius had to act quickly and decisively to save the battle for his side. He had himself been wounded in the mêlée but still fought on. Riding into the midst of the confusion he tried to rally his men. Gesturing to get his men's attention he called on them to come to him and continue the fight. He would lead the next charge in person. His target was the unit of exposed Roman archers, which continued to pick off – and demoralize – the German warriors. Arminius managed to stem the retreat of men and corral them. Surrounded by his loyal retainers he gave the order and the German warriors, gripping their shields and wielding their *frameae*, began a new assault.

The Roman *sagittarii* were now running low on ammunition. Once it was exhausted they would have to rely on their hand-weapons to defend themselves. As they assessed their predicament, the foot-archers formed up tightly ready to take the shock of the German charge. When the Germans clashed with their opponents each warrior used the domed or pointed shield boss to punch, and then thrust his *framea* down in a stabbing motion. The archers crumpled under the onslaught. They would have been wiped out had not the *Cohortes Gallorum*, *Raetorum* and *Vindelicorum*, units comprised of mixed cavalry and infantry, arrived in force to relieve them. Their riders rode among the Germans and broke their charge while the Roman foot-soldiers moved in to engage them in one-to-one combat, pitting their own lances against the Germans'.

The ordered lines of Roman legionaries now arrived and forced their way through the wavering crush of hostile and friendly troops. Legionaries implemented the skills they had practised in training. Each man held his shield close so that its curvature and size protected the length and breadth of his torso from neck to knee. When in range the Roman soldier struck out at his opponent using the domed metal shield boss to wind or injure him, then thrust his *gladius* like a bayonet, aiming for the abdomen, groin or legs – any fleshy part of the body in

Many Germanic warriors carried a sword. These reconstructions are based on finds from a grave in Harsefeld, Germany. Both are single-edged weapons intended for slashing and chopping. The blade of the longer sword (bottom) measures 30.1in long and the tang is enclosed by a wooden grip. The simple scabbards are two-part wooden shells held firmly together with iron bands. A baldric attaches to loops offset at the top to ensure the scabbard hangs vertically. (Tony Austin/Project Germani)

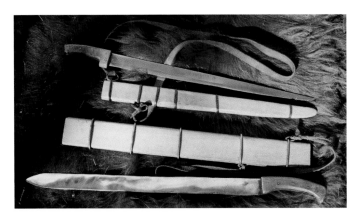

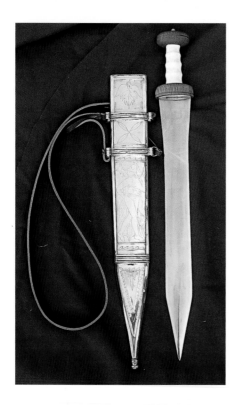

The Roman *gladius* was a two-edged bayonet-like weapon for stabbing and thrusting. This example is based on the so-called Sword of Tiberius in the British Museum found at Mainz, Germany and dated to *c.* AD 15. The iron blade measures 22.6in in length, tapering at the middle and terminating in a triangular point. With the bone grip and wooden guard and pommel the sword weighs 1.8lb. The elaborately decorated scabbard has a core of wood wrapped with tin, with bronze edging and loops to bind it together. (The Ermine Street Guard)

an effort to stall the enemy and provide the opportunity to deliver the *coup de grâce*.

There was a chance Arminius might yet be captured alive. He would make a fine spectacle in Germanicus' triumph if he were taken. It was a fate the Cheruscan war chief wished to avoid at all costs. So that he could not be easily recognized, he smeared his face with his own blood. Then he rode his horse hard and rushed through the Roman lines now closing in on him. He still commanded his opponents' respect, even among the Germanic nations which had sworn allegiance to the Romans. Tacitus writes, 'some have said he was recognized by Chauci serving among the Roman auxiliaries,' adding disapprovingly, 'who let him go' (Tacitus, *Annals* 2.17). Inguiomerus, his uncle, was also at risk of being captured, but he managed to escape the field with his life. For those Germans still in the centre of the conflict, the fight was grim and bloody indeed. In one-to-one combat, ancient warfare was butchery. Superior technical skill in use of weapons could be outplayed by a less able opponent with faster reactions or better stamina.

The tide of battle turned inexorably against the Germans. The trickle of troops fleeing the field turned into a rout. Among the Romans the memory of Teutoburg Pass was still fresh. There, the Germans had treated the Romans with appalling cruelty. Just the previous year the legionaries had buried the bones of their comrades. It was time to settle the score. The victors would show little compassion to the vanquished. 'The rest were cut down in every direction,' writes Tacitus, and

> Many in attempting to swim across the Visurgis were overwhelmed under a storm of missiles or by the force of the current, lastly, by the rush of fugitives and the falling in of the banks. Some in their ignominious flight climbed the tops of trees, and as they were hiding themselves in the boughs, archers were brought up and they were shot for sport. Others were dashed to the ground by the felling of the trees. (Tacitus, *Annals* 2.17)

The report may well contain exaggerations, but there was no convention ensuring that men on the losing side should be treated well once in captivity. Prisoners of war would be treated as slaves, sold to *lixae* and taken back to markets for resale. Depending on his condition a German retainer might serve his days toiling on a farm, or be sent to the school of a *lanista* – such as that discovered at Carnuntum, near Vienna, in 2011 – to be trained as a gladiator for the arena, or endure a worse fate in a mine. While the numbers are not explicitly disclosed in Tacitus' account, Roman casualties were slight compared to the Germans'. 'It was a great victory and without bloodshed to us,' the historian reports, noting 'ten miles were covered with arms and dead bodies' (Tacitus, *Annals* 2.18). The outcome of the clash that day was a clear victory for Germanicus. The failure to capture Arminius, however, would become a lingering headache for the Roman commander.

The Angrivarian Wall

Summer AD 16

BACKGROUND TO BATTLE

As far as the Romans were concerned, by winning at Idistaviso they had won the war. The Roman troops were given permission to pick over the corpses and gather up the spoils. Among them they found lengths of heavy iron chain the Germans had brought with them, so confident were they that they would be taking back live Roman prisoners as slaves. Standing before their general, the troops raised their right arms and acclaimed Tiberius as *imperator* – commander – for bringing them victory. Germanicus then gave the order to pile up the German arms and equipment into a mound, atop of which was set a tree trunk draped like a scarecrow with captured body armour, cloaks, crossed *frameae*, shields hanging from the branches that formed the 'arms', and a helmet on the 'head'. An inscription was affixed to Germanicus' trophy upon which were inscribed the names of all the defeated tribes.

Observing the Romans celebrating from a distance, the Germans seethed with rage. Despite their heavy casualties, they were still many in number and had their weapons. All they needed was another chance to prove themselves. Some did not wait for their war chief to decide but raced off individually or in small bands to attack the Roman troops at will. Many were cut down on the spot or suffered new wounds before retreating back to the German position.

Arminius listened to his men's appeals. He considered his options. Reflecting on his past successes he knew that the Romans were most vulnerable when marching. He could wait for the Romans to leave and launch a repeat of the strategy he had brilliantly executed at Teutoburg Pass; but in AD 9 he had enjoyed the important element of surprise. This time he did not. His men

The Germanic *framea* lance was tipped with an iron blade. Several designs have been found. The reconstructed leaf-shaped blade (left) is based on one found at Görbitzhausen and measures 8.7in. The barbed design point (second right) is a modern copy of a blade found at the Germanic Grave 141 in Putensen and measures 5.5in. (Tony Austin/Project Germani)

This Roman silver *denarius*, minted AD 41–42, shows weapons 'FROM GERMANIA' captured by the Romans as trophies (*spolia*). The archetypal German shield was a narrow hexagon in shape, made of planks of wood, optionally covered with leather and painted, and wholly or in part edged with leather or iron. The central handgrip is clearly visible in the coin. A flag standard is also shown, consisting of a banner with tassels along the lower edge, with an upturned crescent and broad spear blade at the top. Four barbed *frameae* are depicted and two long, straight horns. (Michael V. Craton. Author's collection)

were impatient for action. If he let his own disperse and agreed for the Angrivarii to leave he might not be able to re-assemble so large a force until the next campaign season – for surely Germanicus Caesar would return to build on his victory? While the Romans were in Germania and within his sights he considered that he could bring them to battle again and still defeat them, or at least weaken their resolve to return. His mind was made up. The Cheruscan war chief decided to throw the dice one last time.

He needed to pick his ground well. He found it nearby. It was a wide strip of no man's land marking the border of the territory between the Angrivarii and Cherusci nations. A river flowed past the lower end of the sloping ground, between which there was a marsh. At the top of the rising gradient was forest. He chose *this* place to fight his last set-piece battle against the Roman Army.

Buoyed by Arminius' decision to continue the fight, the men of the Cherusci and their allies, the Angrivarii, assembled by the earthen rampart that normally divided their territories. The Cheruscan war chief gambled that by ordering his men on the entrenchments to rain weapons down upon the enemy, he would slow down the Roman attack; meanwhile, those unprotected by the earthen rampart would hold firm long enough for his cavalry to charge out from the forest and attack Romans on their exposed flank. If the defence failed Arminius could still draw the enemy into the woods where he could repeat the famed massacre at Teutoburg Pass, seven years before. Inside the safety of the enclosure the German warriors patched up their wounds and repaired their kit. Some used the time to attend to their personal appearance, using the shaving kit they carried in their leather belts. Then they waited for the Romans.

Arminius must have hoped to have sufficient time to prepare for the Romans' arrival and to intimidate them with the strength of his fortified location and size of his army – the extent of which is nowhere recorded. However, Germanicus was already aware of his intentions.

His *exploratores* – dispatched to establish the whereabouts of the enemy after Idistaviso – were already spying on the Germans from a safe distance and couriering reports back to him in his camp. 'He was acquainted with their plans,' writes Tacitus, 'their positions, with what met the eye, and what was hidden' (*Annals* 2.20). In possession of the ground intelligence he was able to plan his attack in great detail 'to turn the enemy's stratagems to their own destruction' (Tacitus, *Annals* 2.20). It was particularly important he did so. This would also be his last chance to capture – or kill – his adversary.

Assessing the undulating topology of the site, Germanicus determined that the brunt of the coming battle would, this time, be borne by the legionaries. In particular they were trained to scale entrenchments. He divided up his force into two battle groups. The first, under *legatus* Seius Tubero, occupied the plain. The legions, under their respective legates (the previous year Aulus Caecina Severus had commanded *Legiones* I, V, XX and XXI, Publius Vitellius II and XIV), were placed on the relatively level section of the battle space so they could quickly punch through the German line and pursue the enemy in the nearby forest, supported by cavalry. Germanicus himself commanded the second group, made up of his two Praetorian Cohorts, and assumed 'the especially difficult operation' (Tacitus, *Annals* 2.20) of attacking the enemy on the higher ground. The balance of his army he held back in reserve. Confident of his preparations, Germanicus gave the order to begin the assault.

By standing close together and overlapping shields the Germans could form a continuous defensive wall. With each rank holding its *frameae* pointing outwards the resulting formation presented a dense human 'hedgehog' in the manner of a Greek phalanx. When the Germans enjoyed the added advantage of height – such as from the earthen rampart at the Angrivarian Wall – the Romans found the wall of lances and shields difficult to penetrate. The raised iron boss could itself be used as an offensive weapon, to punch the enemy before striking him with a spear, sword or club. (Tony Austin/ Project Germani)

MAP KEY

1 Early afternoon (approx.): Having gathered at an earthen rampart, the men of the Angrivarii under Inguiomerus form up into a continuous shield wall along the top.

2 Early afternoon (approx.): Arminius and his Cherusci retainers form up on the high ground with the forest behind them.

3 Early afternoon (approx.): The Roman forces deploy by legion and cohort before the Germanic ditch and rampart. Seius Tubero, commanding the forces in the plain, gives the order for the forward units to move against the earthen wall. The legionaries on the level ground quickly break through the Germanic defensive barrier.

4 Early afternoon (approx.): Tubero orders part of his army to march on the level ground into the forest and engage the enemy hiding there. There they encounter resistance from the Germanic side.

5 Mid-afternoon (approx.): On the rising ground, the Angrivarii use their shield-wall formation and long spears successfully to repel the direct Roman assault.

6 Mid-afternoon (approx.): Tubero orders the Roman units attempting to take the middle section of wall to withdraw.

7 Mid-afternoon (approx.): Roman archers, stone slingers and artillery are brought up within firing range of the Germanic position. Missiles rain down on the defenders. Suffering casualties, many Angrivarii pull back out of range.

8 Mid-afternoon (approx.): The Roman bombardment ceases and the assault by the legionaries resumes. The Romans now take the middle section of wall.

9 Mid-afternoon (approx.): Germanicus Caesar leads his two Praetorian Cohorts in a direct attack. Inguiomerus rallies the Angrivarii to repel the invaders. Germanicus' men break through the barrier.

10 Late afternoon (approx.): Caesar wheels his troops round to face the Germans retreating into the cover of the forest. Arminius rallies his men to resist. Packed among the trees, neither side can fully employ its preferred combat doctrine to full advantage.

11 Late afternoon (approx.): Caesar issues orders for one of the reserve legions withdraw from the battlefield to build a camp before nightfall.

12 Very late afternoon (approx.): Caesar removes his helmet so his men can see him in the thick of the mêlée. His men respond to the gesture and rally to him. Inguiomerus drives his men to fight on, but Arminius' resolve is broken. The remaining Angrivarii and Cherusci retreat from the battle space, using the trees and undergrowth to cover their escape. Germanicus Caesar claims victory.

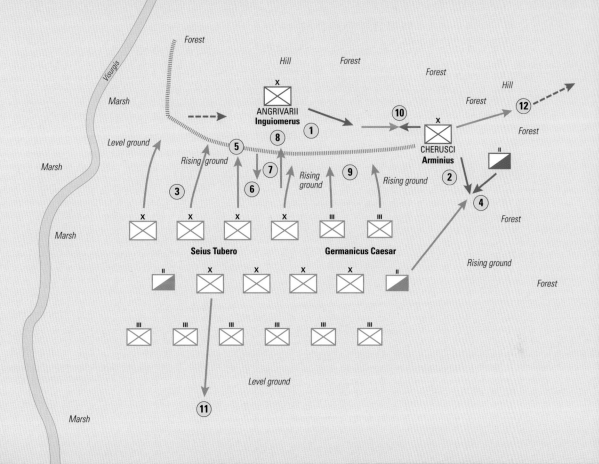

Battlefield environment

Tacitus describes the site of the battle as 'a spot closed in by a river and by forests, within which was a narrow swampy plain' adding 'the woods too were surrounded by a bottomless morass' (*Annals* 2.19). The rampart and ditch (*agger*) may have been a temporary structure hurriedly erected by the Angrivarii just for the last battle between Arminius and Germanicus Caesar or it have been a permanent landmark forming 'a boundary between themselves and the Cherusci' (Tacitus, *Annals* 2.19), built long before the war. Within reach of the site of the battle of Idistaviso, the river mentioned by Tacitus is generally assumed to be the Weser or one of its tributaries, such as the Aue, though the Roman historian mentions Germans retreating to the Elbe further east.

The battle is generally believed to have taken place in Lower Saxony. There are several theories for the location of the actual site of the battle. One places it in the area east of the Weser known as the Hannoversche Moorgeest, between the Steinhuder Meer, a lake 19 miles north-west of Hanover, and the Deister. As was most of ancient Germany in the 1st century AD, this area is still covered by a forest of beech, oak and spruce. Another theory proposes a place closer to the river, at the modern town of Leese. However, on account of the earthen rampart found there, the excavated site beneath the Kalkrieser Berg has also been suggested as the site of the battle of the Angrivarian Wall.

The site of the Angrivarian Wall still remains a mystery. The Hannoversche Moorgeest in Lower Saxony – a gently rolling landscape between Hanover and Nienburg – may be one possibility. It features the largest lake of north-western Germany, called the Steinhuder Meer, which covers an area of 12 square miles and has a shallow basin with an average depth of only 4½ft. Much of the surrounding area used to consist of raised bogs, as shown in this 16th-century map drawn by Johannes Krabbe. (Public domain)

INTO COMBAT

On Germanicus' mark, the *cornicenes* sounded their horns and Tubero's group marched towards their assigned target. They covered the level ground quickly and were soon engaging the Germans. The Germanic shield wall took the shock of the direct wedge charge but the Romans' thrust proved stronger and overwhelmed their opponents' defence. The Roman soldiers directed to take the rampart, however, immediately faced difficulty. Elevated several feet above them, the Angrivarii stood close together, interleaving their shields into a continuous wall of wood and iron. From their higher position they pelted the assailants unrelentingly with missiles. Some Germanic warriors threw their *frameae*, hoping to score a direct hit; others thrust and retracted their lances furiously to push the enemy back. To deflect the projectiles, the legionaries had to approach with their shields up above their heads. Under the heaviest fire centuries approached in *testudo* formation, offering the men maximum protection. Then they had to cross the V-shaped ditch. Designed to slow down an attacker, it was a killing zone. When they made it to the footings of the rampart, they then had to scale its steep side. As the legionaries attempted to climb the slope with their shields held high, the turf of the steep side gave way under their weight and their *caligae* sank into the soft soil, causing some to lose their balance or slip backwards, adding to the difficulty of their climb. Faced with the determined response of their Germanic opponents, the centurions barked out orders to their men to stay close and keep their shields up. Despite their repeated attempts the Romans could not scale the wall. The Germans were successfully holding their defensive formation.

From his vantage point Germanicus surveyed the progress of the battle. He could see that on the level ground his men had pushed back the Germans, but it was evident that progress at the earthen barrier had stalled; in places his men were actually being repelled. The Romans needed to change their tactics quickly in order to take their objective. Germanicus dispatched a messenger to Tubero. Soon after, the curved bronze horns sounded the order the legionaries rarely heard in battle – to withdraw. The legionaries cast a quick glance at their *signa* to confirm it. The centurions barked out the order, no doubt with some relief that the commander had recognized the difficulty of their situation. Continuing to hold their shields up, the legionaries made their tactical withdrawal.

Dodging the German missiles and bodies of their own side on the ground, other legionaries trained as medics scurried to the aid of their wounded comrades. Named after the box of medical supplies they carried, the *capsarii* cleaned the wounds and bandaged cuts on the spot. Those needing barbed weapons to be extracted or broken bones reset were carried to a field hospital set up in the camp. The 1st-century AD writer Aulus Claudius Celsus recorded that, by pouring vinegar directly into the wound, the flow of blood could be staunched (*On Medicine* 5.26.21–24). For a severe wound he recommended placing wool soaked in vinegar and pouring oil over it. He also wrote how, if a wound could not be stitched, the skin could be pinned together with a suture or a brooch (*fibula*), which was typically cast of bronze. (Copper – accounting for about 88 per cent of the alloy – has since been found to have antimicrobial qualities.)

Against the seemingly unbreakable German shield wall ranged against him on the earthen barrier, Seius Tubero called up his artillery – aptly named *tormenti* in Latin. Powered by skeins of twisted gut or horse hair, the *catapulta* was a versatile torsion weapon capable of firing a bolt perhaps 1,200ft – depending on the size and weight of the projectile, the wind direction, the ambient temperature and humidity, the elevation of the weapon and its torsion – with remarkable accuracy. The pyramid-shaped iron tip of the 12in bolt could puncture a hole in a wooden shield, penetrate deep into flesh and smash bone. A trained team could load and fire a projectile every 15–20 seconds and with 59 such machines per legion, a massed array of such weapons could lay down a lethal field of near-continuous fire. The *carroballista* was a catapult mounted on a two-wheeled cart pulled by a donkey or mule, which could be moved across the battlefield to position it closer to the target. Under the withering assault the Angrivarii withdrew, momentarily creating a window of opportunity for the legionaries to launch an escalade. (The Ermine Street Guard)

Germanicus would now turn to the fearsome power of missiles to break the resolve of the defending Germanic warriors. First, units of slingers (*funditores*) were brought forward. Dressed in just a tunic, each slinger carried a leather bag full of ammunition and a sling. His sling was made of non-elastic material – braided flax, hemp or wool – between 2ft and 3ft 3½in long with a cradle about mid-way along its length. One end of the sling – the retention cord – had a loop for the finger. The *funditor* loaded the ammunition – a sling bullet – into the cradle. The best bullets (*glandes plumbeae*) were lead, cast in two-part moulds – usually by the slinger himself – and measured typically just under 1½in long by ¾in wide, and weighed approximately 1oz. The other end of the sling was the release cord, which he held between his index finger and thumb. The *funditor* stood 60 degrees away from his target. He swung the loaded sling in a circular motion in an under- or overhand throw. When content that he had the right rotary speed and aim, he then let go of the release cord. A skilled slinger could hit a target more than 1,300ft away. The sound of whistling of slingshot filled the air accompanied by thuds as the *glandes* ricocheted off the Germans' wooden shields. Others elicited screams of agony as the missiles pierced flesh and struck bone. A bullet striking the head could concuss or kill a man.

In the meantime the *praefectus castrorum* had ordered the artillery (*tormenti*) to be brought up by the artillerymen (*libritores*). *Carroballistae* were mounted on wheeled carts pulled by mules for mobility. These massed weapons of destruction – each legion had up to 60 artillery pieces – used the energy stored in torsion springs of twisted skein or horsehair held in place in a wooden frame (*capitulo*) strengthened by iron plates. The spring bundle could be tightened by adjusting washers at the top and bottom. A rigid wooden bow arm was lodged in each of two springs. The two arms were joined together by the bowstring. One *libritor* locked the bowstring under

'Like scaling a wall'

Seen through the eyes of a Roman soldier, a century of legionaries is shown the moment before the unit is ordered to pull back after their assault against the Angrivarian Wall fails. The plan had seemed simple enough. The legions positioned on the level ground under legate Lucius Seius Tubero would advance and storm the earthwork (*agger*) defended by warriors of the Angrivarii nation. The unit depicted here, led by its centurion, had marched up in close order. At his command, when within firing range the soldiers unleashed a volley of *pila* to clear the way forward or at least to push the enemy back so the legionaries could climb the rampart.

The Romans have seriously underestimated their adversaries. Smarting from their defeat at Idistaviso, the Germans are a motivated force. Standing closely side-by-side with their shields overlapping, the Germanic warriors form a dense wall of wood, iron, flesh and bone and are determined to repel the enemy. The Germans absorbed the opening enfilade. In front of them the massed ranks of legionaries have advanced, but the Romans must first cross a V-shaped ditch running the length of the entrenchment. The Germans' plan is to repel the army of Germanicus Caesar before it can gain a foothold on their redoubt. Using their higher vantage point the Angrivarii use their long lances to stab at the enemy to keep them away, and swords to cut and clubs to bludgeon anyone who comes in too close.

Under a storm of sharp projectiles and deadly thrusts of Germanic *frameae*, the trench has become a killing zone. 'Those who had to assault the earthwork encountered heavy blows from above, as if they were scaling a wall,' writes Tacitus (*Annals* 2.20) a century after the event. The heavily equipped Roman infantry – some wearing chain mail shirts, others the newer segmented plate armour – have to hold their shields above their heads for protection, which reduces their forward visibility and makes the ascent harder. Trying to scramble up the steep side of the earthen bank, some of the men have to crawl on their hands and knees as the soil crumbles under their hobnailed boots in places.

Despite repeated attempts by the legionaries to climb up the embankment, the Germanic defence has proved too strong. 'The *legatus* saw how unequal this close fighting was,' writes Tacitus (*Annals* 2.20); in the next few minutes Tubero will order his men to withdraw.

an iron or bronze claw affixed to the slider. The other used levers on a winch attached by a rope to the slider to draw it back like a crossbow. A ratchet acted to keep the mechanism in 'safe mode' while being primed. The action of pulling back the slider built up greater torsion in the spring. When it had been pulled back far enough, the first gunner placed a sharp or bolt into the slider. The second *libritor* aimed the catapult by swivelling it up and down and side to side on its pivot. When satisfied he had found his target, he pulled back the trigger that released the claw. This freed the bowstring, propelling the projectile with it. A trained artillery crew could fire a bolt every 15–20 seconds with a maximum range of 1,500ft, though the effective distance would be much shorter for picked targets. 'Spears [*hastae*] were hurled from the engines' (Tacitus, *Annals* 2.20), and the damage caused by the enfilade was immediate.

The Germans had no technology available to counter such weaponry, but they would not give up so easily, even under intense fire. As the Roman historian notes, 'the more conspicuous were the defenders of the position, the more the wounds with which they were driven from it' (Tacitus, *Annals* 2.20). The combination of these long-range terror weapons had the desired effect. The Germans tried to stand up to the hail of bullets and sharps but, taking heavy casualties, they finally pulled back out of missile range. The legionaries were ready. When the enfilade ceased, exploiting their enemy's momentary disarray, the legionaries charged again at the rampart. This time they rushed up the embankment, clambered over it and engaged the returning Germans. Even Inguiomerus' urgent attempts to rally the men were not enough. Now the advantage had shifted to the Romans and they pushed back their opponents.

As the legionaries grabbed control of the entrenchments on the plain below, Germanicus now led his own assault at the head of his Praetorian Cohorts against his section of the rampart. Seated on his horse and resplendent in his commander's panoply of muscled cuirass and military cloak, he was a highly conspicuous figure. Exchanging his officer's distinctive sword (*parazonium*) for a cavalryman's *spatha*, he raised his right arm and signalled for the men to move forward. The elite of the Roman Army advanced with determination upon the earthen barrier. Seeing the Roman commander approaching, the Germans redoubled their struggle. Here was the chance to win glory in the eyes of their fellow warriors and before their war chief Arminius. The ensuing hand-to-hand fighting was intense and bloody. The Praetorians, however, proved the stronger force, cutting down anyone standing in their way, and scaled the wall.

Having lost their fortified position, the Angrivarii and Cherusci now fell back. Tacitus notes that 'a morass was in the enemy's rear' and that the Romans 'were hemmed in by the river or by the hills' (*Annals* 2.20). 'Both were in a desperate plight from their position,' he writes; 'valour was their only hope, victory their only safety' (*Annals* 2.20). However, Arminius' choice of location meant his men could still withdraw to the cover of the forest and regroup there. The fight was not over, but his strategy was not without its problems. In the confined space the Germanic warriors could not wield and swing their long *frameae*. Even so, in the Germans' favour neither could the Roman legionaries fight in mass formation with their short *gladii* and heavy shields between the close-spaced tree trunks.

The legionaries moved in, navigating the soft, uneven ground and thick trunks of the trees. Egged on by their centurions they headed forward. The Germans, too, faced their enemy with grim determination. At this point the styles of fighting between the Germanic and Roman troops were similar. The warrior used his domed iron shield boss to push his opponent like the legionary did, lunging with his machete-style sword or bone-crushing club. The legionary took the blows with his curved *scutum* and replied with a thrust of his double-edged *gladius*. It was a duel in which luck as much as skill could determine who lived. In the thick of battle, as the stress of command and the pain of his wound took its toll on him, even Arminius' resolve began to falter. His uncle, Inguiomerus, rode among his men trying to rally them to push the Romans back. He was a respected warrior in his own right; many responded to his rally cry and charged again at the enemy.

The battle was not yet lost by the Germans, but neither was it won by the Romans. Germanicus knew the outcome now hung in the balance. So that his men could see his face, Germanicus ripped off his helmet and tossed it aside. He shouted to the men around him, exhorting them to fight on. They would not yield, he is reported to have said; they would take no prisoners, but continue the slaughter until the Germanic nations were completely destroyed. Then he charged into the fray. Seeing him personally engaged in the fight with their own eyes, and despite being weary and bloodied, the regular Roman troops cheered and resolved to win

While there were professional foot-archers (*sagittarii*), Roman legionaries were also trained to use the bow. Vegetius recommends trainees should be taught 'to hold the bow in a proper position, to bend it with strength, to keep the left hand steady, to draw the right with skill, to direct both the attention and the eye to the object, and to take their aim with equal certainty either on foot or on horseback' (*On Military Matters*, 1.15). The Roman bow was made from horn, wood and sinew laminated together. Compared to a 'self bow', constructed from a single piece of wood, the recurve-design composite bow is smaller but gives higher draw-weight in the early stage of the archer's draw, storing more total energy for a given final draw-weight. Many copper-alloy and iron arrowheads have been found. Surviving arrows from Dura Europos and Qasr Ibrim show the fletching was glued and the shafts were reed, wood or a combination. (The Ermine Street Guard)

Lucius Seius Tubero

The (adopted?) son of Lucius Seius Strabo (*praefectus* of Egypt) and brother of Lucius Aelius Seianus, Lucius Seius Tubero (*c.* 24 BC–*c.* AD 40) ascended the public career ladder and became 'an upstanding citizen and a personal friend' of Tiberius Caesar (Tacitus, *Annals* 4.29.1). In the German Wars under Germanicus he served as *legatus legionis* and led an army group at the Angrivarian Wall. Like all legates of the time, his appointment was a personal choice of the emperor. Augustus set the term of service at two years but under his successor the posting often lasted longer, usually three to four years.

A senior officer like Seius Tubero would wear body armour such as depicted in this marble trophy from the Gardens of Sallust, Rome. Dating to the close of the 1st century BC, it is comprised of an anatomically correct muscled cuirass; debate continues as to whether this type of armour was metal or leather. It was worn over a leather or linen 'arming doublet', the ends of which were slit into a fringe (*pteryges*) for mobility. The cloak is tied at the shoulders. (Marie-Lan Nguyen/CC BY 2.5)

the battle for their commander. 'Our soldiers,' writes Tacitus, 'with their *scuta* pressed to their breasts, and their hands grasping their sword-hilts, struck at the huge limbs and exposed faces of the barbarians, cutting a passage through the slaughtered enemy' (*Annals* 2.21).

The Germans continued to stand their ground, but it was gradually becoming more and more evident that victory was slipping away from their grasp. 'The Germans were equally brave,' writes Tacitus, 'but they were beaten by the nature of the fighting and of the weapons, for their vast host in so confined a space could neither thrust out nor recover their immense *hastae*, or avail themselves of their nimble movements and lithe frames, forced as they were to a close engagement' (*Annals* 2.21). The persistence of Germanicus' troops prevailed, however. Reluctantly, Arminius and Inguiomerus gave up the fight and slipped away from the battlefield. With them went the survivors of the armies of the Angrivarii and Cherusci.

When the last of the warriors had fled, the Romans cheered their hard-won victory. Germanicus called his men together and praised them for their courage, fortitude and loyalty. He ordered them to gather up the Germanic war spoils from the battlefield and to erect another trophy. Upon the pile of captured arms and armour they attached an inscription. It proudly announced:

AFTER THOROUGHLY CONQUERING THE NATIONS
BETWEEN THE RHENUS AND ALBIS,
THE ARMY OF TI[BERIUS] CAESAR,
DEDICATED THIS MONUMENT
TO MARS, JOVE AND AUGUSTUS.

(Tacitus, *Annals* 2.22)

Inguiomerus

Inguiomerus, AKA Inguiomer, of the Cherusci was brother of Segimerus and uncle of Arminius. Tacitus reports that 'his influence with the Romans was long-standing' (*Annals* 1.60.1), perhaps going back to a treaty negotiated with Tiberius in 7 BC. It came as a big disappointment to Germanicus when he learned that Inguiomerus had allied himself with his nephew in AD 15. He had the respect of his allies and enemies. At Idistaviso the Chauci fighting with the Romans recognized him, but let him pass unchallenged. He was a valiant fighter, 'flying through the whole line' (Tacitus, *Annals* 2.21.2) to rally his men at the Angrivarian Wall, despite wounds he had sustained. The year after the battle he fell out with Arminius and joined forces with Marboduus of the Marcomanni in opposition to his nephew.

Respected by friend and foe alike, Inguiomerus was a man of principle, the kind of barbarian the Romans could do business with. Germanicus was bitterly disappointed when he learned the uncle of Arminius had abandoned his Roman allies to support his nephew. Despite gallant efforts to rally his men at the Angrivarian Wall he fled the field, like this man on Trajan's Column. (Conrad Cichorius, 1896)

As Tiberius' deputy and aware of the political sensitivity of doing otherwise, Germanicus omitted his own name and title: the victory at the Angrivarian Wall belonged entirely to his commander-in-chief.

In the immediate aftermath there was a score to settle. The Angrivarii had sworn an oath to Rome as an ally. They had broken the treaty. The Romans took such matters gravely. As a warning to the other Germanic nations who might be tempted to follow their example, Germanicus dispatched Stertinius with orders to take cavalry and crush the Angrivarii. Word of the approach of the Romans reached the allies of the Cherusci. As soon as they entered their territory the Angrivarii promptly surrendered. It was a wise move on their part. By offering their surrender voluntarily to Germanicus Caesar they were able to seek and secure his clemency (*clementia*). A tenet of Roman foreign policy was that it was better to make a friend of an honourable enemy, who might one day prove of value, than to annihilate him. For Germanicus, too, it was a favourable outcome. To get home he would still need to traverse the territory of the Angrivarii. They could yet prove unreliable, but they only needed to keep their word until the Romans had reached the safety of their camps on the Rhine before winter set in.

The return journey proved a particularly treacherous one. Part of the army was sent over land and reached its destination safely. However, the bulk of Germanicus' force had to go by sea. His fleet was still berthed at the mouth of the River Ems. The legions boarded the transports and sailed into the

The troops returning to the Rhine by sea faced a terrifying ordeal. Once away from the safety of the River Ems their lightly built craft – similar to the reconstructed Oberstimm 1 named *Victoria* – were swept away by a sudden violent storm. Many sank with their crews, some were blown off course and landed in Britain, while yet others were shipwrecked on the Frisian coast. Fortunately, many managed to get back to their winter camps with harrowing tales to tell. ("Imperium Konflikt Mythos. 2000 Jahre Varusschlacht". © agenda/Wolfgang Huppertz)

Roman standards depicted by Wenceslaus Hollar, 1653. In the closing weeks of the campaign of AD 16 a second eagle standard was recovered from the Marsi when their chief Mallovendus surrendered to Caius Silius. Combined with the *aquila* of *Legio* XIX rescued by Lucius Stertinius from the Bructeri the previous year, two of the three were brought back by Germanicus Caesar. The third of Varus' lost eagles was finally found among the Chauci and retaken by chance in AD 42 during a mission ordered by then Emperor Claudius, Germanicus' young brother. (University of Toronto Wenceslaus Hollar Digital Collection)

Wadden Sea. There a storm blew up. The fleet was scattered. Some ships were lost, others were blown far out to sea. 'Horses, beasts of burden, baggage, were thrown overboard', writes Tacitus, 'in order to lighten the hulls which leaked copiously through their sides, while the waves too dashed over them' (*Annals* 2.23). A few of the vessels smashed onto the German coast, stranding their men. *Praefectus Equitum* Albinovanus Pedo, who commanded a unit of Frisian cavalry, wrote an evocative poem about the treacherous voyage, which still survives in part.

Only Germanicus' sturdily built trireme survived unscathed, reaching the territory of the Chauci. There the Roman commander bewailed the fate of his men, blaming himself for the calamity. The survivors patched up any damaged ships they could salvage and used their own cloaks and tunics to replace the torn sails. Even the Angrivarii honoured their word. They paid ransoms to secure the return of the Roman soldiers who had been taken captive by the inland nations and handed them over. Yet other ships and their crews had been carried away to the island of Britain. Their kings sent them back across the English Channel, wanting nothing to do with them, perhaps fearing their captivity would be a pretence for a repeat of Iulius Caesar's invasions six decades before. Upon their return, those soldiers told extraordinary tales. 'Every one, as he returned from some far-distant region,' writes Tacitus, 'told of wonders, of violent hurricanes, and unknown birds, of monsters of the sea, of forms half-human, half beast-like, things they had really seen or in their terror believed' (*Annals* 2.24).

Word of the tragedy that had befallen the Roman army on its homeward journey spread across Germania. Some of the German nations saw this as a chance to make war on Rome again. Learning of their intentions, Germanicus dispatched Caius Silius with 30,000 infantry and 3,000 cavalry to launch a pre-emptive strike upon the Chatti, the unswerving allies of the Cherusci. He himself led an army against the Marsi, devastating their country as he traversed it. Their chief, Mallovendus, surrendered to Germanicus and revealed where he could find another of the eagles taken from one of Varus' legions. It was the second of the three lost at Teutoburg Pass that he reclaimed for Rome. (The third eagle was recovered from the Chauci by Emperor Claudius' legate Publius Gabinius in AD 42, according to Cassius Dio (*Roman History* 56.8.7). Astonishingly, some 40 years after Teutoburg, while *legatus* Publius Pomponius Secundus was campaigning in Germania, by chance he rescued several Roman survivors of Varus' army (Tacitus, *Annals* 12.27) who had been enslaved by their captors.)

The resilience of the disciplined legionaries in the face of extreme adversity made a deep impression on the hardy Germanic warriors. Tacitus recounts the response of terrified Marsian prisoners: 'The Romans, they declared, were invincible, rising superior to all calamities; for having thrown away a fleet, having lost their arms, after strewing the shores with the carcasses of horses and of men, they had rushed to the attack with the same courage, with equal spirit, and, seemingly, with augmented numbers' (*Annals* 2.25).

Analysis

Arminius won at Teutoburg Pass and Weser River, while Germanicus Caesar was victorious at Idistaviso and the Angrivarian Wall. While it could be said the final tally was a draw, when Tiberius suspended further campaigns in Germania Magna, Arminius effectively won the war. How a lightly equipped army of Germanic tribesmen could stand up to the full-time, better-equipped force of Roman troops continues to fascinate and intrigue modern students of military history. Examining how the Germans and Romans approached the same conflicts in terms of their leadership skills, objectives, strategies, tactics, combat doctrine and other factors, helps explain the reasons for the outcomes.

LEADERSHIP

Striking are the similarities as much as the differences between the three commanders. When they clashed at Teutoburg Pass, Varus was 55, Arminius 27. Varus was a general with experience gained in several theatres of war and in each he had been on the winning side. The period sources suggest Arminius was a charismatic leader, while Varus is portrayed as vain and arrogant. The Roman commander had proved he could win in a straight fight. His mistake this time was to be too trusting of his Germanic deputy – even refusing to believe intelligence from a respected source that Arminius was a traitor to the Roman cause – and wander right into his adversary's carefully prepared trap.

In Germanicus, however, Arminius met his match. When they clashed at Idistaviso Arminius and Germanicus were separated in age by just one or two years. Both were battle hardened. Both led from the front. They might have served alongside each other in the Balkans during the Batonian War. Even with deep knowledge about Roman strategy and tactics, Arminius could not decisively defeat his contemporary on the battlefield. On the attack the charismatic Germanicus used his knowledge of the wily Cheruscan to outwit

Tiberius Caesar was a commander of note, having seen action in several theatres of war, including Germania. A disciplinarian, he was nevertheless considered a fair general and liked by his troops. Older brother of Drusus the Elder, he was picked by Augustus as his successor. A reluctant emperor – ruling AD 14–37 – he preferred diplomacy over warfare to resolve conflicts with Rome's neighbours. Having allowed his deputy and adopted son to wage war across the Rhine, he finally refused Germanicus' request for a troop surge for AD 17. His decision to abandon Germania effectively made the River Rhine the permanent north-western frontier of the Roman Empire for centuries. (© Karwansaray)

him. Germanicus' failure lay in not anticipating how Arminius would pursue and harass him on his return to the base camps and other operational planning blunders. It was the losses caused by these that eventually tipped the Roman commander-in-chief's position on the future of the region.

The Romans were also well served by the pool of experienced officers, bold and capable of operating independently, upon which they could draw – men such as Lucius Stertinius. Serving under Germanicus as a *praefectus* of cavalry (Tacitus, *Annals* 2.11), Lucius Stertinius was sent to punish the Angrivarii who had defected to Arminius, and in the ensuing battle was dispatched to distract the Germans ahead of the main thrust by Chariovalda, and rescued the Batavians who subsequently found themselves surrounded. At the Angrivarian Wall he was tasked with a flanking attack on the Cherusci. During a raid on the Bructeri he recovered 'the eagle standard of *Legio* XIX lost with Varus' (Tacitus, *Annals* 1.60.3). Fittingly, he received the surrender of Segimerus – father of Arminius – at Ara Ubiorum.

MISSION OBJECTIVES AND STRATEGIES

In AD 9 Arminius' intention was to annihilate the Roman Army and to destroy its ability to exercise command and control in Germania Magna. He convinced the leadership of his own nation not only to combine with their neighbours in a grand alliance, but to do so under his own command. Creating a credible deception, the Germans then degraded the Romans' military capabilities over a period of days using the techniques of the insurgent. Crucial to the success of the deception was the trust between Arminius and Varus. To spring the initial attack Arminius had to sustain the belief that he would return with help. He had no intention of doing so, of course. Finding himself enmeshed in the trap, Varus' initial strategy was to keep his force together and march on. As the situation worsened the Roman goal changed to reaching Fort Aliso as soon as possible, and the baggage train was abandoned in the interests of a speedy escape. When help did not arrive, facing the reality of his hopeless position, Varus committed suicide. Every man was left to save himself.

In AD 16, the situation was very different. Germanicus was on the offensive. His mission was to capture or kill Arminius in the wake of his treachery and the massacre at Teutoburg. The Roman commander first sought to disable Arminius' strongest allies – the Bructeri and Chatti – and in so doing to reduce the Germans' fighting strength in absolute numbers. Aware that the Germans used raids and ambushes, he then moved fast to launch a main thrust against the Cherusci, intending to compel Arminius to committing to a set-piece battle in which he would beat him.

Arminius, meanwhile, was forced onto the defensive. Victory for him would be to stay alive with as many men as he could save. Cut off from his allies, he persuaded the Angrivarii to defect from the Romans to bolster his numbers. He blocked and tackled the invader, attempting to wear down Germanicus' army with surprise ambushes. That strategy failed. Rather than retreat and draw his adversaries into pointless route marches, he boldly decided to face the Romans on the open battlefield. Perhaps he believed he had a real chance of beating his opponent. Encouraged by the German win at Weser River, Arminius assembled his men at nearby Idistaviso. There, his mass charge failed to overwhelm the Romans and the Cheruscan leader was forced to withdraw. Yielding to his men's pleas for a chance to redeem themselves, Arminius took up a defensive position at the Angrivarian Wall. After an initial struggle Germanicus managed to breach the entrenchments. Letting Arminius get away was *his* folly. While Arminius lived he could continue to be a rallying point for anti-Roman resistance. A better strategy for Germanicus might have been to use overwhelming force against one tribe at a time, then hold the gains and gradually extend the reach with successive campaigns – precisely as his father Drusus the Elder had done.

PLANNING AND PREPARATION

The Romans fatally underestimated Arminius both as a strategist and a tactician. Evident from Roman accounts is that Varus took no precautions on the return journey to the winter camps. He assumed, with good reason, that the province of Germania was at peace in AD 9. Basic route-march protocol was relaxed, which exposed the Romans to unnecessary risk. In contrast Arminius had prepared his ruse in intricate detail. Alliance partners disabled Roman security posts ahead of the main attack. The decoy worked brilliantly to draw in the Romans and the trap was sprung. As word of its success spread, new allies joined Arminius' cause. Ironically, Arminius' mistake in AD 16 was not being able to destroy the Romans on their march home. He knew this was his enemy's greatest vulnerability yet did not plan to assemble sufficient forces to repeat what the Germans had done so devastatingly at Teutoburg.

Germanicus was well prepared to take Rome's war of vengeance to Arminius. He invaded Germania with fully a third of Rome's entire citizen fighting force and allies. A frontal attack by land neutralized the Bructeri and Chatti. An amphibious landing brought men and matériel from the rear deep into the country of the Angrivarii and Cherusci. Having won the pitched

battles, however, Germanicus made poor decisions about how best to leverage his victory. Rather than establishing a presence in Germania – as his father had done – he brought his men home. Poor planning was then revealed, despite the lessons that should have been learned from the campaign of AD 15. His troop transports were in the wrong locations, and men and matériel were lost in getting to them. Any future campaign would involve having to rebuild the expeditionary army and retake the enemy territory. It was a blunder noted by the emperor.

TACTICS, COMBAT DOCTRINE AND WEAPONS

The battles in Germania demonstrated both the strengths and weaknesses of the Roman legionary. He was an expensive asset and his deployment in battle was carefully considered by his commander. At Weser River he stood and watched as cavalry rescued the Batavian cohorts from encirclement by Germanic infantry. At Idistaviso he played a largely secondary role to archers and mixed auxiliaries. Only at the Angrivarian Wall did the legionary do what he did best: scaling entrenchments and bludgeoning his opponent. Legionary arms, armour and combat doctrine were optimized for the set-piece battle, but they could prove to be inadequate in warfare characterized by hit-and-run ambuscades, especially on the march – as at Teutoburg – where the legionary was particularly vulnerable. To have a chance to win the Romans needed their opponents to come out into the open, and time to prepare.

Archers, artillery, *auxilia* and cavalry would often be used first to soften up the enemy before the legionary was sent into the fray. The legionary relied on dense, disciplined formations to fight, such as the wedge charge, which required physical space – lots of it. His armour was comparatively heavy. After the initial charge to break the enemy line, combat took the form of shoving and stabbing bouts that quickly exhausted a man after a few minutes. Continually relieving tired troops by rotating in fresh men from the rear to the front row was crucial to winning a battle.

In the Germanic warrior the Roman legionary met a formidable opponent. The battles discussed here demonstrate that the professional soldier on the German side was a well-trained, battle-hardened, combat-ready and motivated fighter who was willing to take extraordinary personal risks. He excelled in irregular warfare – ambushes, raids and petty warfare. In an ambuscade the lightly armed Germanic fighter could decisively defeat a heavily equipped legionary by using surprise and terrain to his advantage. In a set-piece battle the German could stand up to the Roman's discipline and formations for a while, but in close-quarters combat the advantage eventually shifted to the legionary, as at Idistaviso and the Angrivarian Wall.

The German's best strategy was to move the battle space from out of the open. If the legionary could be drawn into a forest or pass, the odds could be tipped in the German's favour, allowing him to use the trees and ground vegetation to reduce the available space and, with it, his opponent's ability to deploy in formation. Then his own agility and speed could be applied, with fatal effects upon the disoriented and weary enemy. Arminius knew this well. He always chose to fight close to a forest, usually with one behind his forces, so that even a retreat could offer the possibility of a counter-attack.

In this asymmetric warfare the Germans largely used the strategies and tactics of the guerrilla or skirmisher; the Romans used the strategies and tactics typical of armies fielded by Mediterranean societies. Yet the men of *barbaricum* proved they could fight competently that way too: the Germans' own primary mass formation – the shield wall – could be a formidable defence against a direct frontal attack – especially when combined with entrenchments, as at the Angrivarian Wall where, on one section, the Romans needed artillery to break it. Even with their advantages in agility, stealth and knowledge of local terrain, however, the Germans seemed unable to replicate their decisive victory at Teutoburg Pass in AD 15 and 16. This was largely owing to a failure of Arminius' leadership rather than of the Germans' fighting skill.

Aftermath

In the final analysis the Roman commander-in-chief took the decision to end the war in Germania. Tiberius had personal experience of making war across the Rhine. He had fought in its forests and on its plains with mixed results, and lost his younger brother there. The Romans had certainly suffered major military setbacks before. The *Clades Variana* was not Rome's greatest defeat as is often portrayed – Arausio (105 BC) and Carrhae (53 BC) were far worse disasters. Normally the Romans rebounded; Rome's response to Teutoburg was no exception. As Augustus' then deputy, Tiberius was sent to deal with the matter but, initially, he did not lead a massive counter-attack. Instead, he stabilized the Rhine and led largely symbolic raids across the river.

Shortly after succeeding Tiberius as emperor in AD 37, Caius (who hated his nickname Caligula) marked the 20th anniversary of his father's triumph in Rome on 26 May AD 17, which celebrated his victories in Germania, with a commemorative coin. The commander Germanicus Caesar is shown riding the *triumphator*'s four-horse chariot. On the other side he is shown in a magisterial pose, wearing the full panoply of a senior officer and clasping one of the legionary eagles retrieved during his German Wars, flanked by the words 'STANDARDS RETURNED, GERMANS DEFEATED'. (Michael V. Craton. Author's collection)

The German War of AD 15–16 was Germanicus' conception. Initially a way to restore unit cohesion after a demoralizing legionary mutiny, it became a campaign to defeat Arminius. Tiberius seems to have been willing to let the war take place, perhaps considering the time to be right for launching a new offensive. Despite the victories, the disastrous return to the Rhine at the end of both the second and third seasons soured Tiberius' mood towards the project. He rejected Germanicus' appeal for more time and a troop

Arminius was a potent figure of resistance against the full might of the Roman military machine in his own day and has since attained semi-mythical status right down to our own times. However, ruling over his people as a king, he came to be seen as a tyrant by many, including his uncle, Inguiomerus, who deserted him in protest. According to Tacitus he 'fell by the treachery of his kinsmen' (*Annals*, 2.88) aged 37. In the 16th century Martin Luther reinvented the Cheruscan chief as a hero for a new emergent Germany and renamed him Hermann. This colossal 87ft statue of him, which stands in the Teutoburger Wald near Detmold, was erected in 1875. (Daniel Schwen/ CC BY-SA 3.0)

surge for a campaign in AD 17. He would no longer tolerate the losses in blood and treasure for only marginal gains. Germanicus relented, and accepted a triumph in recognition of his victories, a second consulship and the post of governor general in the East.

As emperor, Tiberius adopted an approach of strategic patience, preferring to conduct proxy war through Rome's Germanic allies, rather than direct intervention, in order to keep potential threats to her interests in check. Had he acceded to Germanicus' wishes, Tiberius' forces could – some say would – have retaken Germania. That outcome would have changed the course of world history. Instead, the Rhine became Rome's *de facto* north-western frontier and the legionaries withdrew to camps along the left bank to guard against incursions of Germanic warriors from the other side.

BIBLIOGRAPHY

Ancient sources

Caesar, *Commentaries on the Gallic War*. Caius Iulius Caesar (*c.* 100–44 BC) was the consummate Roman commander and is famous for his third-person debriefing report on the wars to conquer the nations of Aquitania, Belgica and Gallia Comata. In his account he describes his encounters with the German tribes and the wooden bridge he threw over the Rhine.

Cassius Dio, *Roman History*. Lucius (or Claudius) Cassius Dio (*c.* AD 155 or 163/164–after AD 229) was a senator and consul who dedicated 22 years of his life to writing a history of Roman civilization from the legendary arrival of Aeneas in Italy after the fall of Troy to the reign of Emperor Alexander Severus. Written in Greek in 80 volumes, Book 56 is one of the best sources for the events occurring before, during and after the battle of Teutoburg Pass.

Celsus, *On Medicine*. Aulus Cornelius Celsus (*c.* 25 BC–AD 50) was an encyclopaedist who is best known today for his work on medicine, pathology, pharmacology, orthopaedics and surgical techniques in Roman times. His recommendations on treating wounds provide insights into techniques used by medical personnel on the battlefield.

***Corpus Inscriptionum Latinarum* (*CIL*)** is a collection of Latin inscriptions. It is an authoritative source of public and personal inscriptions, which throw light on all aspects of Roman life and history. The *CIL* is comprised of 17 volumes in about 70 parts, recording approximately 180,000 inscriptions from the territory of the Roman Empire, arranged by geography. The Berlin-Brandenburgische Akademie der Wissenschaften regularly updates and reprints the *CIL*.

Crinagoras, *Palatine Anthology*. Crinagoras (or Krinagoras) of Mytilene (70–18 BC) was a poet and ambassador. One of his 51 epigrams congratulates Tiberius Caesar on his military victories in Germania, and another preserves the memory of Arrius who tried to prevent his legionary eagle from falling into the hands of the Germans at Teutoburg.

Florus, *Epitome of Roman History*. The identity of Iulius Florus (or Lucius Anneus Florus or Publius Annius Florus), who lived during the 2nd century AD, continues to be debated. In two books, the *Epitome* summarizes all the principal wars fought by Romans up to his time of writing and is one of the few extant sources for the battle of Teutoburg Pass.

Josephus, *Jewish War*. Yosef Ben Matityahu or Titus Flavius Josephus (AD 37–100) was the former leader of the resistance at Yodfat (Jotapata) during the First Jewish War of AD 66–73. He surrendered to the Romans and prospered, writing several books in Greek under his Roman name. His *Jewish War* is valuable for the observations it gives of the Roman Army at war in the 1st century AD.

Pedo, *At Sea in Germania*. Albinovanus Pedo, who lived in the late 1st century BC–mid-1st century AD, was a *praefectus equitum* in charge of a unit of Frisian cavalry in Germanicus Caesar's army during the campaigns of AD 15 and 16. A fragment of his evocative poem about the sea voyage is preserved in Seneca the Elder's *Suasoriae* 1.15.

Pliny the Elder, *Natural History*. Caius Plinius Secundus (AD 23–79) began his career as a soldier in the Rhine army, seeing three tours of duty (AD 45–51), including one as a *praefectus equitum*. The *Natural History* in 37 books is a compendium of knowledge in the mid-1st century AD, covering the world and the elements – the natural world of plants and animals as well as the world created by man, including its nations and peoples, cities, art and architecture inside and outside the Roman Empire.

Strabo, *Geography*. Strabo or Stravonos (63/64 BC–*c.* AD 24) was a historian, geographer and philosopher. He is best known for his *Geography*, a descriptive survey in 17 books of the world known to the Romans. In it he details the nations of ancient Germany and includes a list of captives displayed at Germanicus Caesar's triumph in AD 17 to celebrate his victory over the Cherusci and their allies.

Tacitus, *Annals*. Publius (or Caius) Cornelius Tacitus (AD 56–117) was a senator who wrote several books during the reign of the Emperor Trajan. The work known as the *Annals* (or *From the Death of the Divine Augustus* to give it its correct title) details the events of the reigns of Tiberius, Caligula, Claudius and Nero. It is our only source for the wars of Germanicus Caesar in Germania (AD 15–16), including the battles of Weser River, Idistaviso and the Angrivarian Wall.

Tacitus, *Germania*. The book *Concerning the Origins and Location of Germania* is Tacitus' summary of contemporary knowledge about the lands and peoples on the right bank of the Rhine and Danube in the mid- to late 1st century AD. It is one of the most important sources of information about Germanic culture and war fighting.

Vegetius, *Epitome of Military Matters*. Publius Flavius Vegetius Renatus wrote a treatise in the 5th century AD on army reform, usually referred to today simply as *On Military Matters*, in which he described the training regimen of the army of the early Roman Empire. He explains how an army should fortify and organize a camp, train troops, handle undisciplined troops, handle a battle engagement, march and many other topics.

Velleius Paterculus, *Roman History*. Caius (or Marcus) Velleius Paterculus (*c.* 19 BC–*c.* AD 31) served under Tiberius, first in Illyricum as a *praefectus equitum* during the Batonian War, and then in Germania as a *legatus legionis*. His *Compendium of Roman History* is one of the few sources for the battle of Teutoburg Pass.

Modern sources

Adler, Wolfgang (1993). *Studien zur germanische Bewaffnung: Waffenmitgabe und Kampfesweise im Niederelbegebiet und im übrigen Freien Germanien um Christi Geburt*. Hochschulen des Saarlandes. Bonn: Habelt.

Austin, Norman J.E. & Rankov, N. Boris (1995). *Exploratio: Military and Political Intelligence in the Roman World from the Second Punic War to the Battle of Adrianople*. London: Routledge.

Bishop, M.C. (2002). *Lorica Segmentata. Volume I: A Handbook of Articulated Roman Plate Armour*. JRMES Monograph No. 1. Duns: The Armatura Press.

Bishop, M.C & Coulston, J.C.N (2006). *Roman Military Equipment From the Punic Wars to the Fall of Rome*. Oxford: Oxbow Books.

Bowman, Alan K., Champlin, Edward & Lintott, Andrew, eds (1996). *The Cambridge Ancient History: Volume X – The Augustan Empire, 43 B.C.–A.D. 69.* 2nd Edition. Cambridge: Cambridge University Press.

Clunn, Tony (1999). *In Quest of the Lost Legions: The Varusschlacht*. Gillingham: Arminius Press.

D'Amato, Raffaele & Sumner, Graham (2009). *Arms and Armour of the Imperial Roman Soldier From Marius to Commodus, 112 BC–AD 192*. Barnsley: Frontline Books.

Dreyer, Boris (2009). *Arminius und der Untergang des Varus: Warum die Germanen keine Römer wurden*. Stuttgart: Klett-Cotta.

Erdkamp, Paul, ed. (2010). *A Companion to the Roman Army (Blackwell Companions to the Ancient World)*. Oxford: Blackwell.

Freese, Heinz Dieter (1997). 'Neues vom Angrivarier-Wall', *Berichte zur Denkmalpflege in Niedersachsen* Vol. 17, No. 3: 138–41.

Hegewisch, Morten (2012). 'Von Leese nach Kalkriese? Ein Deutungsversuch zur Geschichte zweier Erdwerke', in Ernst Baltrusch, Morten Hegewisch, Michael Meyer, Uwe Puschner & Christian Wendt, eds, *2000 Jahre Varusschlacht. Geschichte – Archäologie – Legenden*. Berlin: De Gruyter: pp. 177–209.

Johne, Klaus-Peter (2006). *Die Römer an der Elbe. Das Stromgebiet der Elbe im geographischen Weltbild und im politischen Bewusstsein der griechisch-römischen Antike*. Berlin: Akademie Verlag.

Kornemann, Ernst (1980). *Tiberius*. Frankfurt: Societäts Verlag.

Le Bohec, Yann (1994). *The Imperial Roman Soldier*. London: B.T. Batford.

Lendering, J. & Bosman, A. (2012). *Edge of Empire: Rome's Frontier on the Lower Rhine*. Rotterdam: Karwansaray.

Murdoch, Adrian (2006). *Rome's Greatest Defeat: Massacre in the Teutoburg Forest*. Stroud: Sutton.

Oorthuys, Jasper, ed. (2009). *Ancient Warfare Special 1: The Varian Disaster*. Zutphen: Karwanarsay.

Powell, Lindsay (2011). *Eager for Glory: The Untold Story of Drusus the Elder, Conqueror of Germania*. Barnsley: Pen & Sword Books.

Powell, Lindsay (2013). *Germanicus: The Magnificent Life and Mysterious Death of Rome's Most Popular General*. Barnsley: Pen & Sword Books.

Roth, Jonathan (1994). 'The Size and Organization of the Roman Imperial Legion', *Historia: Zeitschrift für Alte Geschichte*, 43.3: 346–62.

Schlüter, Wolfgang (1999). 'The Battle of the Teutoburg Forest: archaeological research at Kalkriese near Osnabrück', in J.D. Creighton & R.J.A. Wilson, eds, *Roman Germany: Studies in Cultural Interaction*. Journal of Roman Archaeology Supplement 32. Portsmouth, RI: 125–59.

Schönberger, H. (1969). 'The Roman Frontier in Germany: An Archaeological Survey', *The Journal of Roman Studies*, Vol. 59 (November): 144–97.

Schoppe, Siegfried G. (2006). 'Varus fand sein Ende im Lippischen Wald. Eine Streitschrift wider die Kalkrieser Hypothese' (http://www.arminius-varusschlacht.de/varus-kalkriese.pdf, accessed 8 September 2013).

Schuchhardt, Carl, Bersu, Gerhard, Heimbs, Georg, Lange, Hans (1926). 'Der Angrivarisch-Cheruskische Grenzewall und die beiden Schlachten des Jahres 16 nach Chr. zwischen Arminius und Germanicus', *Praehistorische Zeitschrift*, Vol. 17: 100–31.

Seager, Robin (1972). *Tiberius*. Berkeley, CA: University of California Press.

Speidel, Michael P. (1983). '*Exploratores*: Mobile Élite Units of Roman Germany', *Epigraphische Studien Sammelband*, Vol. 13: 63–78.

Speidel, Michael P. (2004). *Ancient Germanic Warriors: Warrior Styles From Trajan's Column to Icelandic Sagas*. Abingdon: Routledge.

Strassmeir, Andreas & Gagelmann, Andreas (2009). *Das Heer des Arminius: Germanische Krieger zu Beginn des 1. nachchristlichen Jahrhunderts*. Berlin: Zeughaus Verlag.

Syne, Ronald (1933). 'Some Notes on the Legions under Augustus', *The Journal of Roman Studies* 23: 14–33.

Tilmann, Bechert (2003). *Römische Archäologie in Deutschland. Geschichte, Denkmäler, Museen*. Ditzingen: Reclam Verlag.

Timpe, Dieter (2006). *Römisch, germanische Begegnung in der späten Republik und frühen Kaiserzeit. Voraussetzungen – Konfrontationen – Wirkungen. Gesammelte Studien*. Munich: K.G. Saur Verlag.

Wamser, Ludwig (2000). *Die Römer zwischen Alpen und Nordmeer*. Düsseldorf: Albatros im Patmos Verlag.

Watson, G. R. (1969). *The Roman Soldier*. London: Thames & Hudson.

Wells, Colin M. (1972). *The German Policy of Augustus: An Examination of the Archaeological Evidence*. Oxford: Oxford University Press.

INDEX

References to illustrations are shown in **bold**.